A Cast Iron Community

The Story of Burnbanks

Bampton & District Local History Society

www.bampton-history.org.uk

Published by
Bampton & District Local History Society
2006

ISBN 978-0-9554862-0-3

Foreword

By the Rt Hon David Maclean
Member of Pariament for Penrith and Borders

There are arguments whether it was right or wrong to flood the lovely Mardale valley with its isolated rural community to make the Haweswater reservoir. But there can be no arguments about the vision of Manchester Corporation to create the model village of Burnbanks to house the transient workers who were building the dam. These days it would be portacabins or caravans and indeed most other temporary accommodation at the time consisted of tin huts and cheap houses. But Manchester wanted something substantial and decent in keeping with its vision of building a great new city. Therefore they selected cast iron as a building material which would not only withstand the Lakeland weather but would subsequently have good re-sale value.

The end result was a model village which not only housed workers and their families but provided excellent recreational facilities, even a dispensary and a mission hall as well as their own front door, garden and, at that time, state of the art facilities such as electric lights, hot and cold water, a bath and an indoor toilet. There was, in fact, a village atmosphere – a community – with workers living amongst families where they could be nourished in body and soul, unlike the navvies of previous projects whose transient lives and temporary housing were not so conducive to respectable, civilised living.

This fascinating book documents the lives, hopes and fears of those who worked and lived at Burnbanks and also how the village gradually declined from the 1940s onwards. However, it also records the recent renaissance of the village as a new community to house local people in times when rural housing is very much desperately needed.

I was honoured to be present at the official opening and unveiling of a commemorative plaque at Burnbanks in May 2006 and it is a tremendous privilege for me to be asked to write a foreword for this wonderful book. I must pay tribute to the Bampton and District Local History Society, and especially John Drinkwater, whose painstaking research and vision enabled the history of Burnbanks to be documented and also to those who created a new Burnbanks for the 21st century.

Finally, I would ask you to read the acknowledgements at the end of the book in order to appreciate the remarkable contribution made by many to tell the Burnbanks story through the memories of those who lived and worked there while keeping alive the vision of this incredible project.

David Maclean

Houses of Parliament

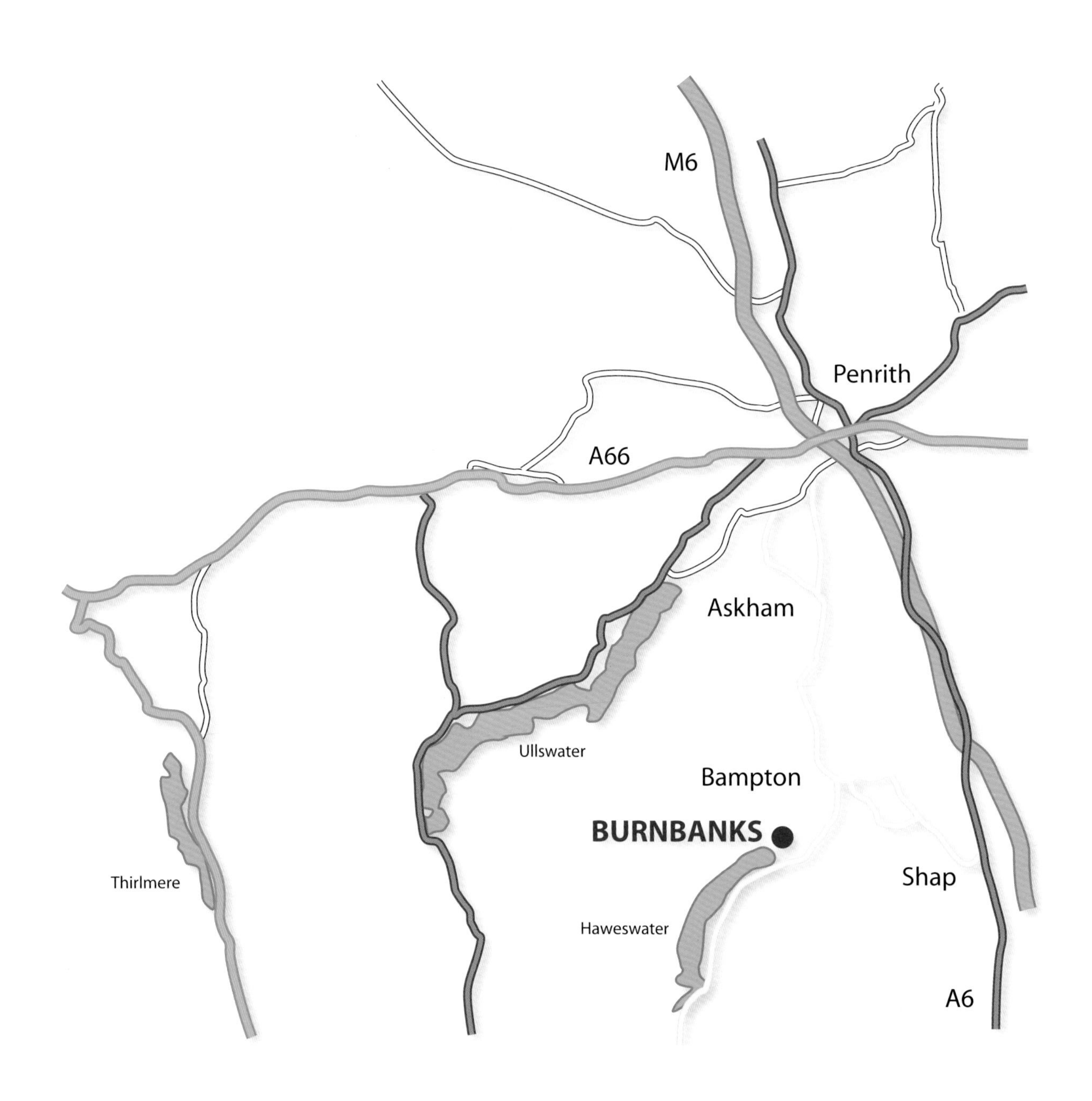
M6
Penrith
A66
Askham
Ullswater
Bampton
BURNBANKS
Thirlmere
Shap
Haweswater
A6

A Cast Iron Community

The Story of Burnbanks

Contents

Haweswater showing the boathouse

It was early in 1933, about February.....

All over the country, men were walking the roads without enough to eat looking for work. Grown men were begging for sixpences outside every hotel and railway station. Dad was worried; he did not want to sign on for the dole and he was desperate for a place.

Then he got talking to a man who told him there was a chance of a job in the Mardale valley five miles over the hills. This was where the reservoir was to be built to collect the drinking water from the surrounding hills to send through the tunnel to Manchester. Dad was told it was a good rough five miles from Longsleddale to Mardale but if he went round by road through Shap it was easily 20 miles. We had no money for a bus fare and there was no direct bus service anyway so Dad said that he would walk it himself.

He finished work on the Friday night. He wore his old felt hat, an army great coat and some old waterproof leggings. He had a bad limp and he was tired out but he was game. He walked all day Saturday and by evening he was soaked right through to the skin and lost somewhere up near High Street Mountain.

He told us later that he had just given up when he saw a light at a farmhouse down in a valley and more by good luck than anything he scrambled down and staggered up to the door. Fortunately the farmer's wife was a kindly soul and she took him in and dried him off and gave him a meal.

He was given a lift in a cart down the valley while he slept and he presented himself to the Foreman Manager Mr. Johnson and asked for a job on the Sunday morning. Mr. Johnson was a Scotsman and he said "Any man who would walk over the mountains for a job damn well deserves one".

However he could only put him on digging foundations in the hole at the bottom of the works to start with. They were not supposed to take anyone on for other work until the whole dam work was started in several weeks time. So for weeks Dad worked with a pick and shovel with all the navvies. Then he was put to work in the power station.

And Mum and I were sent for in a lorry and all our bits and pieces were brought to the village of Burnbanks, to live at No 5.

Mrs Mairghread Sharp (nee MacColl), from a written account sent from her home in Queensland, Australia

The original Haweswater

Introduction

Despite four years of war and continuing suffering, 1919 felt like the threshold of a new era. World War One had been the 'war to end all wars'; the power of science and the march of democracy promised new ways of tackling problems, not least poverty and ill-health. There was confidence that society's troubles would be re-examined and that fresh thinking would bring exciting improvements. The 1920s dawned as a 'new age' where old conventions could be overturned in the passion for modern ideas, styles of dress, music, dance and above all, building and architecture.

Manchester was one of Britain's most 'progressive' places – a city that relished its pioneering role and seized every opportunity to promote the improvement of its economy and its citizens. Disillusion followed as financial difficulties mounted and new ideas foundered. Manchester had to modify many of its aims, but the hope of creating a better city remained. In the 1920s and 1930s, the Haweswater Dam was one of Manchester's most ambitious and novel projects designed to secure essential water for people and industry. The associated Burnbanks village was a visionary settlement, where transient workers in an isolated Lake District valley would find everything they needed for civilised living.

This book tells how Manchester's vision for Burnbanks fared. Using accounts of people who lived and worked there, it relates the village's creation, occupation, consolidation, decline and redevelopment between the years 1919 and 2006.

Looking towards an undeveloped Burnbanks from Mardale

The sacrifice of a remote and idyllic valley and the homes and way of life of a few people who lived in it to provide the water needed to safeguard the future prosperity of a great industrial city makes a compelling story. But the story is not simply history – it still lives. Until recently there were many people who had known Mardale before the flood and were willing to tell anyone who would listen of its peace and beauty. There were also a few who had lived there, were even born there, and who, after 40 years were so affected by what had happened to them that they refused to speak of the subject. They have now died but their silence is remembered and speaks more eloquently of the sadness for their lost world than anything they could have said.

It is an emotive story but its broad outline is so well-known it hardly needs re-telling. Bampton and District Local History Society chose to concentrate on a less well-known aspect: not the lives of those who were driven out by the flood but of several hundred people brought in from distant places, often very different in appearance and character, to inhabit the instant cast iron village at the end of the valley and build a dam to create a reservoir. This was happening at a time when the whole nation and much of the world was experiencing ever-increasing unemployment and economic recession.

Many of the workers came with their families while the single men were housed with families. Their employers, the Manchester Corporation Waterworks Committee, calculated that the men would settle more easily, be more manageable and work better if they had a home and family to return to after work and would be a less disruptive influence in the pubs of the nearby quiet village of Bampton and in Penrith which was more distant but at the end of a regular bus route. They had often left behind grim living conditions in dangerously overcrowded and insanitary slums but where there was the comforting familiarity of neighbours they knew and often an extended family. Now they had been uprooted and put down in a hostile wilderness, without pavements, street lights or cinemas with only sheep as close neighbours. They would not have perceived the Lakeland landscape as a rural paradise as the 19th century Romantics did but more as the 17th century travellers thought of it: composed of barren rocks and horrible precipices. There was a powerful incentive for these 'settlers' to get to know each other quickly and to bond themselves into a close community. They must also have been very conscious of being watched from a mile away by an initially incompatible and uncomprehending village.

As a community Burnbanks was in a very awkward position. It was temporary. Even its houses were chosen precisely because they could be quickly dismantled to be sold and re-assembled elsewhere. But it was not so temporary. It was going to take many years to build the dam - a significant part of the lives of those who stayed the whole time - but when the job was complete and the reservoir slowly filled up most people and houses had to go. Most of the workers are now dead and the memory of Burnbanks in the 1930s is preserved by the children who came with the workers or were born in the settlement. As childhood memories are often the most vivid we are fortunate to have been able to locate people from as close as Penrith and from as far away as Australia who spent part of their childhood in Burnbanks. The Bampton and District Local History Society has pieced together the story of the building of the dam but our central theme was always the lives of the people of Burnbanks and they can tell that story best themselves. A number of these former inhabitants have been interviewed and these interviews are the most important part of our book. The fascination is in the detail: the apparently trivial, disconnected scraps of information which give the narrative immediacy, which bring it to life.

& 10 Geo. 5.] *Manchester Corporation Act,* 1919

CHAPTER cxix.

An Act to empower the lord mayor aldermen and citizens of the city of Manchester to obtain a supply of water from Haweswater and other sources in Westmorland to provide for the transfer to them of the undertaking of the North Cheshire Water Company to make further provision in regard to their water and electricity undertakings and for other purposes. [23rd December 1919.]

A.D. 1919.

A copy of the Act of Parliament allowing Manchester to build the Haweswater Dam

Early construction at Burnbanks with the original Haweswater in the background.

Thirst for water and the Haweswater scheme

In the 19th century the population of England doubled twice and there was a dramatic movement from the countryside to urban areas, particularly to the rapidly growing industrial centres in the North. This put a great strain on all basic needs and one of the most urgent problems in the great industrial centres was the need for an adequate supply of clean water. Without it there were severe epidemics of water-borne disease such as cholera and typhoid.

In Manchester, most houses had no running water. People worked on shifts in factories and mills. A dozen people could share one bedroom, and up to a hundred houses shared the one 'privvy' (a hole dug in the corner of a yard), or a 'midden' (a heap against a wall). Sewage was carted off and dumped into a river. Houses were crowded, damp and filthy and rain seeped through walls. Manchester and Salford's slum dwellings became a national disgrace. Engels wrote "The Condition of the Working Class in England" based on the plight of the Manchester poor. Manchester had the highest number of paupers in the whole of Britain - higher even than in London's East End. Clean water was urgently needed to alleviate the dreadful living conditions. Meanwhile there was an ever-increasing demand by industry for more water. Shortage of water could bring many industries to a standstill.

So the new municipal authorities began to embark on ambitious schemes to create reservoirs in mountainous regions where there is heavy rainfall and only small populations to be displaced, and to move the water through pipelines to the greater centres of population. Manchester traditionally got its water from the nearby Pennine slopes, but by the second half of the 19th century its population and industries were outgrowing this source. They looked to the Lake District and decided that Thirlmere could be dammed with a fairly small dam and enlarged to form a large reservoir. There would have to be a pipeline of about 80 miles, a major undertaking which would take many years to complete and they also had to contend with a vigorous campaign of opposition from influential people who loved the landscape and wanted it to remain undisturbed, but the need for water in Manchester was urgent and the scheme went ahead.

Before the Thirlmere scheme was complete it was realised that soon even more water would be needed and that for technical reasons enlarging Haweswater to create another reservoir would have to be the next step. In 1919 the Manchester Corporation obtained an Act of Parliament to build a dam across the end of the Mardale valley so that Haweswater would grow to fill the bottom of the valley for its entire length.

Bampton, the only significant settlement near Haweswater was, and still is, an ancient, scattered, parish devoted almost entirely to farming and related occupations. On the eastern side of the valley are hills and common grazing land and on the west side after some enclosed fields and common ground are higher hills and eventually mountains. The Haweswater Beck flows out of Haweswater, past Thornthwaite Hall, a large old manor house which once had a deer park, and into the River Lowther at Bampton. Near Thornthwaite a gap in the hills leads into the secluded valley of Mardale.

Mardale was a remote place but not unknown to or unappreciated by people from the outside world. From the 19th century it was a favourite destination for walkers, painters and naturalists who stayed at The Dun Bull Inn or in farm houses. There are a number of well-known paintings of the valley and the lake by Jacob Thompson and several of his friends. Lord Lonsdale who was lord of the manor had a boathouse by the lake with a boatman who took people fishing. The lake was also fished with nets to provide food for Lord Lonsdale's family and guests at Lowther Castle, a few miles away.

Beside the road which led along the west side of the lake into Mardale was a bare hillside with rocks and rough grazing for sheep. It was called Burn Banks. The name Burn Banks was given to the proposed pre-fabricated village which was to be erected on the site.

Towards the end of the 19th century farming was declining nationally as cheap produce began to arrive from distant parts of the world, and remote upland places like Bampton were particularly severely affected. Over the past two hundred years the population of Bampton has decreased steadily. While the country's population has grown to more than six times what it was in 1800 the population of Bampton has halved. Everywhere during the 19th century and the early part of the 20th century, people, particularly young people, were leaving villages and migrating to urban centres like Manchester to find work in the factories and mills.

In July 1925, Sir Edward Holt, Chairman of Manchester Corporation Waterworks Committee told an assembled meeting at the George Hotel, Penrith: 'The Haweswater scheme will bring a great watershed to a great city. When Manchester has finished…there will be no more charming spot than Haweswater. In my opinion Haweswater is presently very much over-rated. It will be more beautiful in years to come.'

In 1925 the whole scheme, which was to cost around £10 million, was set out in detail with staff appointed to be responsible for the various parts. The part of the project which concerns us most directly is the actual village of Burnbanks, but we cannot separate it completely from the infrastructure needed to bring materials to and from the site and from catchment areas which were to provide the water for the reservoir.

Manchester acquired more than 22,500 acres of land in the lake's catchment area, mostly from the estates of the Lonsdale family. This included the valleys of Swindale, Wet Sleddale and Heltondale, partly to be able to have some control of the quality of the water going into Haweswater and also because there were plans for two further smaller reservoirs at Swindale and Wet Sleddale to be constructed after the Haweswater dam was completed. The cost of this vast area of land was £175,000, which represented about £7 per acre, including all the farms and buildings on the land. In today's prices the sale price of the land and farms would be equivalent to about £5.5 million.

The subsequent report acompanying the newspaper photograph on the right reads:

'It was at the Stockdale or southern portal of the tunnel that the charge which inaugurated the work was fired by the Lord Mayor. Accompanied by Sir William Kay, Sir William Cundiff, and other members and officials of the Manchester Waterworks Committee, by the Mayor of Kendal and representatives of the Westmorland County Council, he stood under the safe shelter of a ruined building on a low-lying shoulder of Gatesgarth and, by pressing a brass handle, fired a charge of high explosive which dislodged many tons of rock.

Fragments of the rock were hurtled for a great distance over the countryside, and one of these killed a rabbit, which was quietly watching the proceedings from the other side of the valley.

3—THE HERALD, SATURDAY, OCTOBER 25, 1930.

Harnessing Haweswater.

Manchester's Lord Mayor Fires a Blasting Charge.

BIG TUNNEL BEGINS WITH BIG BANG.

Boring Five Miles underneath Mardale Fells.

THE LORD MAYOR OF MANCHESTER (MR. R. NOTON BARCLAY) AFTER FIRING THE SHOT.

Mr. Noton Barclay is seen holding a rabbit, the only casualty of the explosion. Near to him, wearing his chain, is the Mayor of Kendal (Mr. Norman F. Wilson).

Photos by courtesy of the "Daily Sketch."

The chairman and deputy chairman of the Waterworks Committee were to have fired succeeding shots but owing to the torrential downpour this was abandoned and a dash was made for the motor cars which took the party back to Kendal.'

Mr Bill Rawlings, who lived in Burnbanks village from its outset, tells us in his interview about the demolition and clearing at the start of the project: "When they started knocking the farm houses down, well right from the word go it started - I'm just going on reminiscing now because I can't remember this - but they did start taking the timber down before the 30s. So it was always put out there to weather and season and it was actually a big field and it was full during the war. We used to play on it, had little camps in it. The whole trunk come down. Well when I say the whole trunk they would be cut into maybe lengths of eight foot or something like that but whatever sizes they wanted they were. Well next to that was the estate, which is still there, and a saw mill and it was sawed up into fencing, larch bars, gates to serve all the farms because the Corporation bought most of the farms around the area so they had to do all the fencing, all the fencing round the lakes. That was all cut from there - beams for the farm houses and I suppose they did sell quite a bit off."

In 1925, the minutes of the Manchester Waterworks Committee emphasised that the first priority was to create a railway from the main line sidings south of Shap to the site of the dam. There are about 90 large leather bound volumes of these minutes, one for each year from the 1840s, and only one, that for 1926, is missing. The 1927 volume describes progress in building a road from Shap to Burnbanks but we do not know for sure why the railway failed to materialise. The road, known locally as the Concrete Road or the Cement Road is a very well-planned piece of engineering with very strong concrete bridges and carefully constructed gradients to facilitate the passage of big, heavily-loaded lorries. It is also well drained and does not flood when other local roads do. Part of the road's purpose was to divert the heavy traffic away from the local communities of Shap and Bampton where they would have been a nuisance and would have increased hostility to the whole project.

30 MILES OF STEEL TUNNELS.

WATER SUPPLY FOR A CENTURY.

FROM OUR SPECIAL CORRESPONDENT.

LONGSLEDDALE (near Haweswater), Westmorland, Tuesday.

ONE of the greatest engineering feats ever attempted to provide a water supply was set on foot in this wild Lakeland spot to-day.

When the Lord Mayor of Manchester, Councillor Noton Barclay, pressed down the finger in the electric shot-

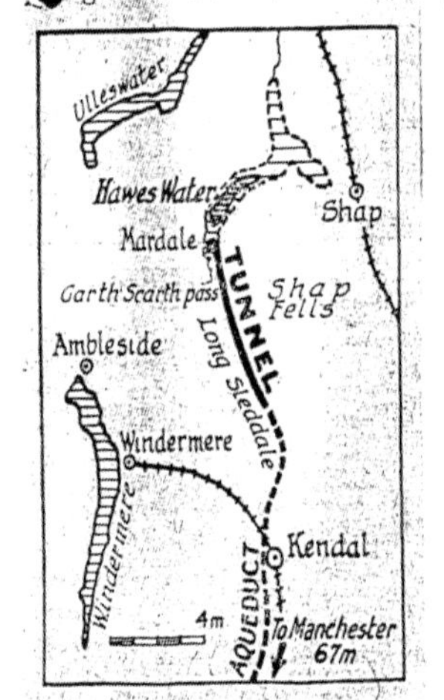

firer shortly after noon 30 tons of volcanic rock was blown 200ft. high.

This was the first shot fired in one of man's greatest battles against Nature. In the course of the struggle to drive a tunnel five miles long and 9ft. in diameter through the iron-hard slopes of a crater that became cold millions of years ago £10,000,000 will be spent by Manchester Corporation to provide the population of the city with more water.

No one can say what the engineers will find when they reach the heart of the great mass of Gray Crag, through which the tunnel will be driven 2,000ft. below the summit.

A WEIRD SCENE.

It was a weird scene that we saw to-day in this forbidding little gorge. Rain was falling in torrents—it has been raining for three weeks almost ceaselessly—and one could scarcely see ten yards. Perhaps it was Nature's gesture of rebellion against the scarring of her grey and green hill slopes.

Her wrath descended upon everyone impartially and soaked us all to the skin by the time we had finished the gruelling toil of climbing a quarter of a mile of steep bogged slopes.

The Lord Mayor, perhaps, suffered more than the rest for he was in full morning dress. The mist dulled the gloss of his silk hat and hung in little drops upon his chain of office. He stood on the top of the steep slope for the tunnel entrance. Here the rock had been stripped of its green mantle of grass like flesh bared before the surgeon's knife.

There was a deep roar which echoed from every rock as the Lord Mayor pressed home the plunger. The veil of mist had lifted suddenly, and we saw thousands of fragments of rock split and fly in every direction, to be caught by a huge safety net which had been placed 200 yards away to prevent the falling missiles from striking the onlookers.

VILLAGE UNDER WATER.

The roar was echoed by a great cheer from aldermen, councillors, officials, and workmen. War had been formally declared against the ancient hills.

The level of Haweswater lake will be raised 90ft. by a great dam. The thousand-years-old church and graveyard at Mardale, together with the school and cottages and farmhouses, will be submerged, and the lake will be increased in length from seven to 10 miles. Next to Windermere Haweswater will be the largest English lake.

Perhaps the most remarkable feature of the undertaking will be that while Thirlmere water is pumped to Manchester that from Haweswater will travel all the way by gravity at the rate of 90,000,000 gallons a day, as it comes from 700ft. above sea level.

The tunnel will run under the high range of mountains which is joined by Shap Fell to the Pennines, and it will lie parallel to the wild foot track 2,000ft. high from Kendal to Mardale which is known as Gate Scarth Pass. It will be lined for 30 miles with steel and stone, and in addition to the water pipes running through there will be space for workmen to carry out repairs at any point.

ARMY OF WORKMEN.

Small villages of huts are already springing up in the green valley to accommodate the army of workmen who will shortly be employed for five years at both sides of the mountain range. At present about 70 men are at work.

The aqueduct will solve Manchester's water problem, it is estimated, for the better part of a century.

Afterwards the Lord Mayor, the chairman of the water committee (Sir William Kay), and about 100 corporation and contract officials lunched at Kendal. The Lord Mayor said :—

"We are confident that we shall be able to carry this £10,000,000 project through without adding a halfpenny to the water rate. Manchester's first water supply was drawn from a spring which is now buried in a street in the middle of the city."

Daily Mail, October 22nd 1930

This Indenture made the Twenty third day of February One thousand nine hundred and twenty three **Between** The Right Honourable James William Viscount Ullswater G.C.B. P.C. The Honourable Christopher William Lowther of 61 Elm Park Gardens Chelsea in the County of London a Major late in His Majesty's Army and William George Frederick Cavendish Bentinck of 78 Harley Street in the said County of London Esquire J.P. (hereinafter called "the Trustees") of the first part The Right Honourable Hugh Cecil Earl of Lonsdale (hereinafter called "the present Earl") of the second part and The Lord Mayor Aldermen and Citizens of the City of Manchester (hereinafter called "the Corporation") of the third part **Whereas** the Trustees are entitled during the life of the present Earl as assignees of his life estate under the Will and Resettlement hereinafter mentioned to the possession of the lands and hereditaments hereinafter described including the hereditaments over which the rights privileges and easements hereinafter described are granted (together with other hereditaments) but upon the trusts declared thereof by a certain Indenture of Settlement dated the twenty fourth day of May one thousand eight hundred and eighty one and made between the Right Honourable St George Henry Earl of Lonsdale of the one part and William Stuart Stirling Crawfurd and James Lowther of the other part and by the Will (hereinafter called "the Will") dated the seventh day of February one thousand eight hundred and seventy six of the Right Honourable Henry Earl of Lonsdale who died on the fifteenth day of August one thousand eight hundred and seventy six and an Indenture of Resettlement (hereinafter called "the Resettlement") dated the eleventh day of November one thousand eight hundred and seventy six and made between the Right Honourable St George Henry Earl of Lonsdale of the first part the said William Stuart Stirling Crawfurd and James Lowther of the second part and the Right Honourable George Augustus Frederick Cavendish Bentinck and Charles Hopkinson of the third part by reference to the Will the Trustees as the present Trustees of the Will and the Resettlement are

Made between Jane Lowes John Lowes and Mark Lowes of the one part and the said James William Lowther and Christopher William Lowther of the other part.

(g) Low Rough Hill Bampton

11th July 1872 **Admittance** of Noble Kirkpatrick Mounsey of this date.

15th May 1888 Indenture of mortgage of this date made between the said Noble Kirkpatrick Mounsey of the one part and Jane Dalton of the other part.

5th October 1897 **Indenture** of Conveyance of this date made between the said Noble Kirkpatrick Mounsey of the first part the said Jane Dalton of the second part the present Earl of the third part and the said James Lowther of the fourth part.

...aled and delivered ... The Right Honourable ...iam Viscount Ullswater ... nce of G. R. Ellis Dankes, 10 Little College Street Westminster S.W. Solicitor — Ullswater

...aled and delivered ... The Honourable ... William Lowther ... ence of J. K. Rigby, 123 Pall Mall S.W. — Christopher W. Lowther

...Secretary to Lord Lonsdale

...aled and delivered ... William George ... Cavendish Bentinck ... sence of J. K. Rigby — W. G. F. C. Bentinck

...aled and delivered ... The Right Honourable ... Earl of Lonsdale ... sence of J. K. Rigby — Lonsdale

16

Two pages from the 20 page Conveyance of property and land for the Haweswater scheme between Lord Lonsdale's Trustees and Manchester Corporation (23rd February 1923)

MANCHESTER CORPORATION WATERWORKS.

HAWESWATER ESTATE.

TO BE LET, with entry on the 25th March 1928.

THE DUN BULL HOTEL, Mardale, with about 42 acres of Meadow and Pasture land.
The Hotel is fully licensed and free from brewer.

GOOSEMIRE AND GROVE BRAE FARM, comprising about 65 acres of Meadow, Pasture, and Arable land, together with a flock of 110 sheep and grazing rights on the Commons for sheep.
The buildings on this holding include:-

GOOSEMIRE.

Dwellinghouse - comprising kitchen, parlour, pantry, wash-house, and three bedrooms.
Byres to tie 12 cattle.
Two-stall stable with loft.
Barn, slaughter-house, and loose box.

GROVE BRAE.

Dwellinghouse - comprising kitchen, parlour, back kitchen, pantry and three bedrooms.
Byres to tie 16 cattle.
Four loose boxes.
Barn, loft, and implement house.

The Hotel and Farm are at present in the occupation of Mr. R. E. Daffurn who resides at the "Dun Bull".

Mr. Alexander Speak of Measand Beck Hall, Bampton, Shap, will show the properties on receiving one day's notice in writing.

The accepted tenant will be required to pay all rates, taxes and outgoings, except Landlords Property Tax; to execute the Corporation's usual form of agreement of tenancy, and, so far as regards the Farm, to enter into a bond for the re-delivery of the flock of sheep let therewith.

The Sporting Rights are in each case reserved to the Landlords.

For further particulars apply to the Engineer, Waterworks Department, Town Hall, Manchester.

Tenders for the respective tenancies endorsed "Tender for Hotel" or "Tender for Farm" as the case may be, and addressed to the Chairman of the Waterworks Committee, Town Hall, Manchester, to be sent in not later than the 30th November 1927.

L. HOLME LEWIS. Engineer.

Burnbanks - a model village

It was agreed that temporary accommodation would have to be provided for those employed on the Haweswater dam project. The Manchester Waterworks Committee was not ready to give its full attention to the construction of its 'model village' until 1929, but when it did it acted very quickly. The plan was to build a settlement on land at the northern end of Haweswater, an area known as Burn Banks.

The committee selected 19 firms which made 'workmen's huts' and asked them to submit tenders. Some did not provide enough details in their tenders and others proposed buildings which were too flimsy for the harsh weather conditions in the area. Of the few which remained as possibilities, all were of wood except one - which was of cast iron. Prices ranged from £800 to £1200 and the cast iron one which they chose was in the middle of the range. The deciding factor was that the committee judged that cast iron buildings would deteriorate less than wooden ones in the harsh Lake District climate, would be more easily dismantled and would have a greater re-sale value. This tender was accepted in June or July of 1929 and work began in September. By the end of the year most of the village was built.

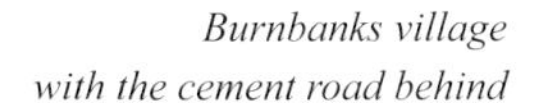

Burnbanks village with the cement road behind

Each house weighed two elephants!!

Manchester built its reputation as the 'shock' city of the industrial age on its civic pride and its shrewd commercial judgement. At Haweswater, it aimed to provide a model of social housing as well as best value for money. Not for Burnbanks then a 'tin town' of corrugated hutments or temporary 'cob' dwellings such as others had provided for reservoir workers in the Pennines or railway navvies at Shap. At Haweswater, Manchester Corporation wanted to build a sturdy village that would embody its grand civic vision.

After World War One there were many attempts to develop new forms of house construction because of national shortages of materials and skilled labour. Cast iron houses had been constructed in the nineteenth century, the earliest on a canal-side in Tipton, West Midlands. By 1920, cast iron was being replaced by newer construction materials especially steel, timber and concrete. Newton, Chambers & Co of Sheffield remained a major provider of cast iron houses. Dwellings using its external cast-iron flanged plates were erected at Derby and Dudley. Each house used 11 tons of pig iron (equivalent to two African elephants) but cost less than conventional brick.

At Burnbanks, the Newton Chambers system showed its flexibility. On a difficult site, the cast-iron houses were quickly erected on minimal foundations. Three types of accommodation – large hostels and one and two bedroom bungalows – as well as a Dispensary and the Mission Hall were built from seven identical types of cast iron component. The various house 'kits' were quickly put together in a few days by unskilled labour. Each cast iron semi-detached house cost between £400 and £500. Their resale value was an important factor in Manchester's decision to use this system.

The cast iron walls were faced with cement while the interior was lined with a thin patent weather boarding. The facilities though gave many occupants exactly what they wanted – their own front door, a garden, electric light, hot and cold water, a bath and an indoor toilet. By the beginning of 1931, 400 workers with their wives and families were housed in these unconventional houses, in some comfort and with many of the necessaries of village life.

But already Manchester's grand plans were beginning to be modified because of financial limitations caused by the worrying state of the national economy. The railway apparently had to be reduced to a road, possibly because of these cutbacks, and a wooden building to accommodate Burnbanks children at Bampton School replaced plans for a whole new school at Burnbanks. At first it was intended that there would be a hydro-electric scheme which eventually became just a little building with an ordinary diesel generator in it. Probably this was not so much because things were costing more than expected but that everywhere national and local government was having to economise and less money was now available. But water was still needed, so economies were made and the scheme went ahead.There were several types of houses but those which remained until recently were of the same design. Other wooden bungalows were built away from the main village for occupation by tradesmen and managers and were more attractive, even incorporating verandahs.

Burnbanks new residents outside their homes

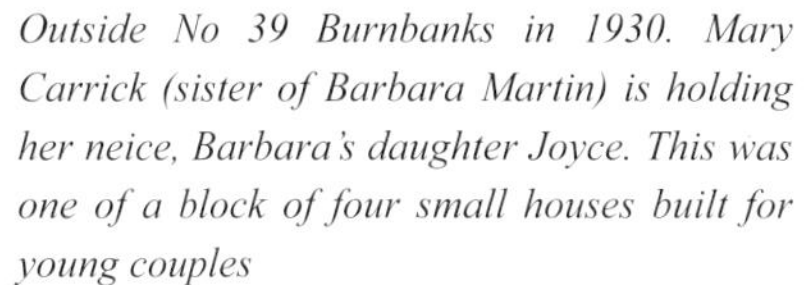

Outside No 39 Burnbanks in 1930. Mary Carrick (sister of Barbara Martin) is holding her neice, Barbara's daughter Joyce. This was one of a block of four small houses built for young couples

Margaret Higson (daughter of Harry and Jessie Astbury) moved to Burnbanks in 1930 at just eight weeks-old. Her father was working on the dam project as an engineering draughtsman from late 1920's. They lived in one of these better quality houses: "We lived in one of the 'top' houses at Burnbanks for a short while before moving to No.2 The Oaks, Burnbanks for roughly five years. My brother George Edward was born while we lived at The Oaks in 1933. There was a long garden behind the house and we loved playing on the outcrop of rocks and further down, a large hen run.

The inside of No. 1 The Oaks where Mr and Mrs Hindmarch lived, before redevelopment 2005

"Home was always comfortable and warm. We ate many meals under the veranda. Mum cooked on either the fire range in the living room - always black-leaded on Fridays - or on the paraffin stove/oven in the kitchen. Mum was a good cook – everything tasty and simple: no need for artificial additions. The Naddle Gate bungalows are still standing (*at the time of her letter*): kitchen, pantry, outdoor coal place in the back porch, living room with a hatch into the front room, bathroom, hall and three bedrooms."

Mrs Eastham, hut 27 (left) and Mrs Bardsley, hut 28, with local children

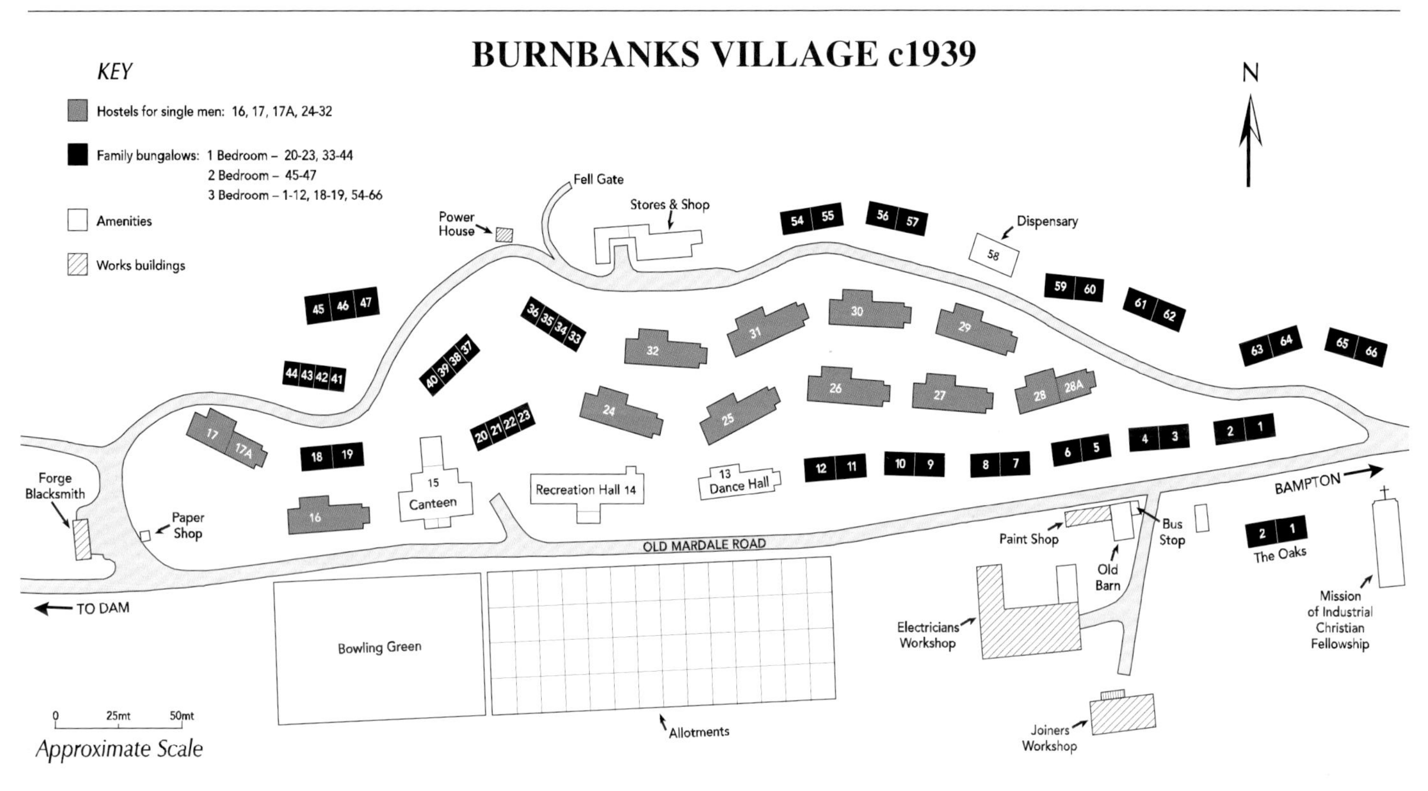
BURNBANKS VILLAGE c1939
KEY
Hostels for single men: 16, 17, 17A, 24-32
Family bungalows: 1 Bedroom – 20-23, 33-44
2 Bedroom – 45-47
3 Bedroom – 1-12, 18-19, 54-66
Amenities
Works buildings
N
Fell Gate
Stores & Shop
Power House
Dispensary
Forge Blacksmith
Paper Shop
Canteen
Recreation Hall 14
Dance Hall
OLD MARDALE ROAD
BAMPTON
TO DAM
Paint Shop
Bus Stop
Old Barn
The Oaks
Mission of Industrial Christian Fellowship
Electricians Workshop
Bowling Green
Allotments
Joiners Workshop
0 25mt 50mt
Approximate Scale

Christmas in Burnbanks 1933

Mum and Dad hoped to have their first Christmas together in their own home. The exhaustion plus the poison that had beset Mum's system was still causing trouble and a week before Christmas she became ill. She had a fever and lay in bed quite unable to walk with extremely painful legs, especially her left hip. It was called acute rheumatism.

Dad worked in the power station looking after the compressors on shift work and he was doing afternoon shift that week but had Christmas night off-duty.

All preparations for Christmas had been made; secret presents wrapped up and although she had been lying quietly on the sofa on the afternoon of Christmas Eve Mum had managed to bake some mince pies and other cakes.

She walked carefully with the aid of a stick to the scullery to see that everything was alright after the stockings were hung up, but she found to her horror that the Christmas duck, which had been hung up by string behind the back door, had fallen on the floor. It was a nice plump duck and falling on the floor would not hurt it but for one thing - the cans which contained the paraffin for lighting the primus stove always stood behind the back door. One can was leaking and the duck was lying in a puddle of paraffin. It had been there some time probably since Dad went out to work slamming the door behind him. She picked it up and realized the bird was covered down all of its body with the horrid smelly stuff, so she put it on some brown paper, left it on the draining board, went back to bed and cried herself to sleep. Dad came home at 7am and on being told tearfully that the Christmas dinner was useless and covered in paraffin, he inspected the damage. Then whistling through his teeth he set to work. He filled a basin with water and soap and plunged the duck into it and then he scrubbed all over again and again and then he rinsed it over and over in cold water. Then he mixed up loads of sage and onions and stuffed the duck and put it in the oven.

At one pm Christmas Dinner for everyone was declared the very best ever!

Mrs Mairghread Sharp

Most of the general workers' homes were for families and even the housing for single men was organised so that a family was attached to each hostel. Employers recognised that a much more stable and manageable work force would result from a family situation rather than from having a few hundred men living 'away from home' in a strange environment. So there were hostels, or boarding houses, made to a different pattern by the same firm. These housed about 12 single men, each with a small separate sleeping cubicle arranged along a corridor and a common living area at one end. At the other end of the building was accommodation for a housekeeper and her family. The husband would be one of the workers on the dam.

The single men who lodged in these boarding houses were an essential part of the workforce; they were real 'professionals'. They had often spent their working lives going from one big work site to the next, living in temporary accommodation with often no settled home to go back to. Many would have lived in other temporary settlements like Burnbanks. They provided the stability in the community and the experience in the workforce.

Most of the workers came from two locations though there were others from a wide range of places. One large group came from Manchester and industrial Lancashire generally. They must have found the alien location, which would have seemed even more remote then than now, a great culture shock. Another large group came from industrial parts of West Cumberland where unemployment was so severe that the Government was prepared to contribute towards the wages of West Cumbrian workers as an inducement to Manchester to employ them at Burnbanks.

Exterior of a big hut

Big hut being erected

Mr Bobby Eastham remembers moving to number 30 at the age of 8 in 1929. This house, and the one they later moved to at number 27, were known as 'big houses' - lodgings for single workers. Mr Eastham's mother was responsible for 13 men. He describes these men: "The people who came there to work were real tough, rough diamonds, rough navvies. They'd walk the roads looking for work. There were blokes like Marmalade Joe, Stafford Dick and Lincoln Bob. They were all hard, tough and when they went drinking they went drinking not for an hour or two days, they'd go for a fortnight. And my mother would go and wake them up of a morning and they'd say 'oh I'll go tomorrow, I'll go tomorrow'. But they never caused any trouble. They were never any trouble.

"Ours was one of the biggest ones (*boarding houses*). As far as I know there was my mother's, there was Thompson's, and there was Sullivan's, then there was Rideout (*and*) Toone's. Five I think, as far as I recollect, big houses.

"My mother was mainly full-time, that was her occupation, looking after these men and looking after our family. And probably her working day was from about five in the morning till about ten at night. And then my mother had girls working for her. There was a girl called Gladys Jackson come to work for her.

"And mother used to look after money for different people. Lincoln Bob, he was a bit of a boozer, I think, and she said 'if you give me your money I'll look after it', and she did. He stayed with her for a long time, Lincoln Bob.

"The chief engineer, Mr Jameson, was on the Prisoners' Aid Society. He helped to get people work. You got people from all over. I know two lads that stayed with my mother they came from Ancoats in Manchester. I think some did come out of prison.

"Easter time and Christmas those chaps went home so our house was nearly empty bar the hardened navvies that didn't have a place to go to. They stayed and my mother provided food for them. Instead of having about thirteen you could have had about four, that's all, at Christmas.

"Yes, it was a hard life for my mother, but she was happy. On a Friday night, that was when she got all the money from the lodgers, I'd take her out for a walk and show her different birds' nests."

Hughie Davins, aged six, was sent to stay at the Easthams 'big hut' for the summer holidays in 1937 and 1938 where his uncle, Stephen Rhodes was in lodgings. He loved his time with them: "The family consisted of Mr & Mrs Eastham and their son Bobby who I think was in his late teens. I don't know what Mr Eastham did but he was always smartly dressed. The bungalow was divided up into three sections, the first was for the living quarters for the family; in the centre where the front door was located was the kitchen and dining room; leading off the dining room was a corridor flanked on either side by sleeping cubicles, so all the men had their own rooms; at the end of the corridor were the ablutions and back door where the men used to come in after work and get washed and changed.

"Mrs Eastham of course used to do all the cooking, and there was a young girl called Joyce Bird who came in to help with the washing and cleaning. I don't remember how many men were there but I think there must have been about a dozen so Mrs Eastham didn't have much time to relax. I believe she and her husband came from London originally, but I remember her with affection as she was always very kind to me.

"The main meal of the day was in the evening after the men came in from work, the men all sat at a long table whilst the family sat at a smaller table across the room, I always sat with the family for my meals."

Margaret Higson also remembers the Easthams, especially Mrs Eastham's baking: "George, myself and Mum used to visit Mrs Eastham who was in charge of one of the big huts. There was a large kitchen and range – she always seemed to be baking. I still use her ginger biscuits recipe."

In an article in *Cumbria* magazine in 2003, Gladys Walker, who worked for Mrs Eastham, described catering for the workmen: "At first we had paraffin lamps for light and all food was cooked on a massive black stove with water heated in a cistern from the same coal-fed stove. It consisted of six rings and a centre one with ovens on either side. The men who lodged with Mrs Esatham were indeed fortunate: she kept a good table. Breakfast consisted of porridge, bacon and egg or sausage and tomatoes, rissoles and potatoes when new ones needed using up. They packed their own lunches as most of them went out for the day. For this cold, sliced meats were put on the table along with pastries and cake. There was always a hot meal at night: often roasts of beef, lamb or pork with vegetables. Meat and potato pies were made in large enamel bowls. There were fruit pies, rice and sago puddings, spotted dick (which was made up of cake which had to be used up with fruit added) – this being a welcome pudding on a cold winter's night. All this along with their laundry cost them 30/- (£1.50) a week."

In 1930, aged 18 months, William Rawlings (also known as Billy Toone) moved to Burnbanks with his widowed mother

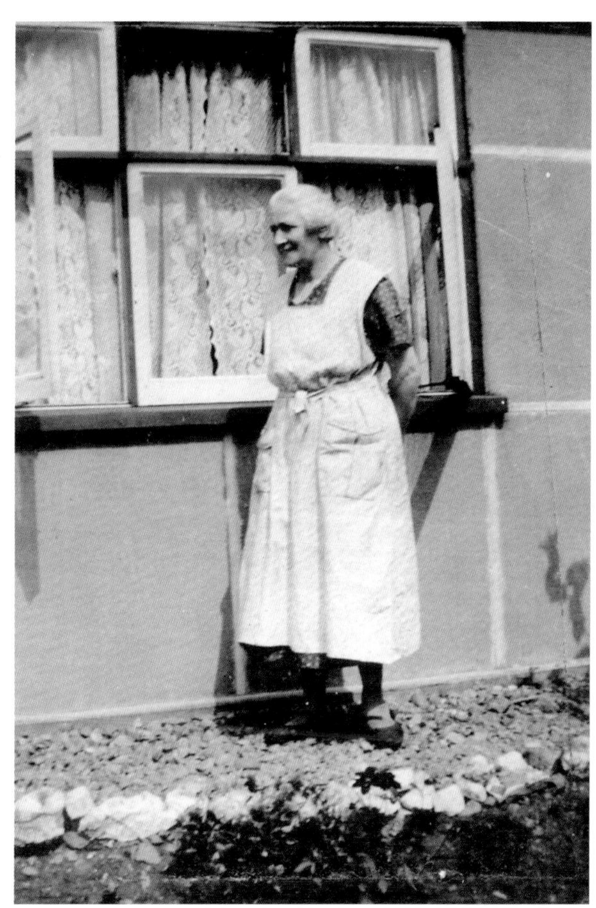

Granny Toone – she looked after about twelve workers at a time in her 'big hut' home

who moved in with her brothers Harry and Bill Toone and sister Ivy Toone. Bill was already working on the tunnel: "So how we all slept I don't know. And then my next recollection was mother getting married again to Bill Twigg and they moved down into number five …into a big hut, that's what they called them - big huts. My grandmother ran it (*the boarding house*). Mary. Mary Jane Toone. And Grandad always called her Polly, I don't know why.

"And I think they had the dormitories. There was the house part - a big living room with a solid fuel range where she used to do all the cooking and that for the lodgers and then behind that there was a sitting room and two bedrooms for Granny and Grandad and Ivy.

"Bill and Harry slept down on the lodgers' side, you know where …. they were wide and then they went narrow and there were dormitories all the way down, just single rooms, and at the end of that there was a little wash place with a little solid fuel fire in again for the navvies, or whatever they were, just to sit at the evening and have a warm and play cards. All the cubicles (were) separate. You had a little single bed, a little cupboard beside it just to put your clothes in and nothing else, that was just about it, and an electric light. Yes you had your own electric light up top to bottom."

Inside one of the big huts, looking from the living room towards the stove and drying area with men's cubicles along each side

No. 1 Burnbanks being built 1929

Billy Rawlings (also known as Billy Toone) with Bill Toone

Staff bungalows at Naddle Gate, note the 'triangle' and the road leading to Burnbanks

"She (*mother or grandmother*) might have done some of the washing for them, I don't know, but they washed their own socks and things like that because down in the bottom, where I said, was this little stove for drying and they were always drying because they were always wet, well not always wet, but they used to come in wet so they had to dry their own stuff off down there.

"Cooking, she had this big - she baked her own bread, made her own cakes and she'd have made quite a bit of bread because she made them breakfast and they took this snack which was cheese, nearly always cheese and corned beef, how they never got fed up of it I don't know, big thick slices, and then they came home to a cooked meal every night. I could even tell you the menu at one time. I know it was pork on Tuesday, beef on Monday, but she varied it - and fish.

"There was a great big table down and benches where you sat on a bench and they used to sit in there and just eat and all the men were down that side and we had the family table on this side. And a great big pot of tea always hot on the range, yes, on top. I would cycle down to Charlie Noble's at Walmgate for a pitcher of milk, take that back up to Granny - to the big hut.

"Monday was wash day. Oh my granny, she did the washing and Ivy helped her out of course and I used to do some drying now and again. On wash days I know I can also remember she had a washing machine - Acdo they called it and you just put your washing in it - mind, she had a big boiler as well but this was the modern thing of the time. It had a handle on with a metal paddle, you closed the lid down, put your washing in, put your hot water in, closed the lid down and just swished it about.

"There was a bath down on the men's side. They could have their bath any time they liked. There was hot water from, I would imagine, an immersion heater, I don't think it was fired from the range - it was electric. That was the only bath. We would bath when they were all at work. Well every Friday night was my bath night anyway. Once a week - now it's every night!

"We had a coal house. There was as I explained the dining room if you like or whatever it was, you went into the living quarters for Granny, a little door on the outside went to the coal house, then next to the coal house inside was the pantry, then there was the washing-up place then you went out another door and there was two outside toilets, outside but inside - you went out of the house and there was two toilets there."

Billy Rawling's uncle, Harry Toone outside their Burnbanks house

In early photographs, the gardens are very stony and rough and generally the whole village looked unfinished as though they couldn't wait to get on with the serious work of building the dam as soon as the houses were fit to live in. The cast iron panels from which the houses were made were clearly visible and only much later were they rendered over. The gardens had to be fenced to keep out sheep but this was done with anything that they could find, often with branches of many shapes and sizes cut from the nearest available trees. There must have been very little time to make the gardens look attractive and PC Ostle's rock garden was not so named because he specialised in rock plants but because it consisted entirely of rocks.

Eric and Alan Jewell playing above the village

Eric and Alan Jewell outside No 65 Burnbanks. Note the makeshift fencing.

Dilys Jewell with Alan and Eric

Living conditions, however, were good at Burnbanks by the standards of the times. They had to be - for employees would not stay contented and prove good workers unless domestic and social life was made tolerable.

The homes at Burnbanks even had electricity. This was provided by a diesel generator in a building which now stands alone in the wood which has grown up between the present Burnbanks and the dam. They probably only had electric lights and not all the other electrical equipment people have today or the power to run it, but at that time no-one else in the area had electricity at all. The houses also had a hot water system and a bath which was important considering the often filthy nature of the work. The earliest houses did not have a proper bathroom but there was hot water from a boiler and the kitchen table could be lifted up to reveal that its base was a bath.

Because there were flushing toilets, there was a sewage treatment plant. Mr Rawlings tells us: "We had a big water treatment place because there were water toilets up there in the village. And there was this big place and this thing used to go round just swinging water round and then of course they'd have to empty the cess pit tanks."

Mr Eastham says: "When we went to live at Burnbanks we used Aladdin lamps for lighting and coal for heating and cooking. Later on, as things got established, they built a power station which housed two or three large generators, providing all the electricity that was required. Those machines were manned 24 hours a day (three shifts of eight hours) and a chap by the name of Jewell was one of those responsible for their smooth running."

One day he was reminded how fortunate the model village residents were with their 'mod cons': "I can remember Bob Holmes (Harry's father) going to work with the horse and cart on the dam. I was talking to him one night. I said 'I'll have to leave you, Bob, I'm going for a bath'.

"He said 'Bath? What's a bath?' He didn't know what a bath was!"

Raymond Holliday was born at number 66 Burnbanks in 1935 and christened in Mardale Church. He remembers the prefabricated three-bedroomed bungalow they lived in as being very cold in the winter. He paints this picture of domestic life: "I think we would eat in the kitchen because the kitchen was quite large. We had electric, we had hot and cold water and a bathroom and flush toilet and the cooking as I can recall was done on a primus stove in the early days. For the washing they used to light a fire in the back kitchen on the boiler for hot water then they would wash in the wash tub with the dolly and then the mangle outside the back door."

The boiler where water was heated for washing.
This picture was taken just before the houses were demolished.

June Nanson, Mr Holliday's sister, came to Burnbanks before her brother was born, just a few months old in 1932. She describes Burnbanks homes: "They consisted of a reasonably sized living room, three bedrooms, kitchen, pantry, bathroom and inside toilet. The ceilings were very high and it was a nightmare when emulsion painting. The walls were very thin and certainly not sound proof. My mum and next door neighbour, Mrs Olive Hindmarch, had many conversations whilst sitting on adjacent loos!"

A couple of Burnbanks characters

Tom Moore moved to Burnbanks in 1926 when he was just six months old. He had two brothers and two sisters, Gordon and Dennis, Audrey and Aletha. They first lived at no 2 Burnbanks: "I don't know how long we lived in it, but the Birds lived in number 1, and they had a fire which spread to our house. And I remember Mam

Fire damage at No 1 and 2 Burnbanks in 1932

HAWESWATER BUNGALOWS DESTROYED.

Two Families' Alarming Experience at Burns Bank.

Burns Bank, the new village near Bampton constructed by the Manchester Corporation for the men engaged on the waterworks at Haweswater, was the scene of a somewhat alarming fire early on Sunday morning, when two families had to make hurried escapes from their burning homes.

The village is composed of bungalows in pairs, and the one nearest Bampton is occupied by Mr. T. Bird and Mr. F. Moore. Soon after two o'clock on Sunday morning Mr. Bird awoke to find that the house was in flames, and he and his wife and two children had to make a very hurried exit. About the same time Mr. Moore heard the crackling of the flames, and he, too, had to take his family to a place of safety.

The bungalows are constructed of iron frames covered with cement, and the interior is lined with a patent wood boarding. In a very short time the woodwork in Mr. Bird's house was burning very fiercely and it quickly reached the adjoining house. The Corporation have fire appliances to be used on the water main which passes through the village, and under Messrs. G. Sandham and W. Bardsley, captain and lieutenant respectively, the brigade attacked the fire with water from a hydrant. Fortunately, the wind was blowing away from the other bungalows, but in view of the restricted nature of the apparatus available it was decided to send for the Penrith Fire Brigade. The latter made the twelve miles' journey to Burns Bank in half an hour—a good run on a comparatively narrow road in the dark—but when they arrived they found that all that was combustible in Mr. Bird's house, including the furniture, had been destroyed, and that the outbreak in the second house was under control. It had, however, suffered extensively, but most of the furniture was saved. The cause of the fire is not known, but it seemed to have originated in the scullery of Mr. Bird's house. The Corporation have their property insured, but we understand that the occupiers are not so protected for their furniture.

The Penrith brigade, which was under Captain Whinray, returned about 5 a.m. The sounding of the fire buzzer at Penrith a second time was due to a defect in the electric bell which gives the warning at the gas works.

and Dad telling us that Jim Fountain, who lived behind us, came down to our house when it was on fire and picked the three of us up in his arms all at once then carried us up to his house. He more or less saved us from the fire. After that we all moved up to number 54, and stayed there until 1944 when we moved into Penrith. They had a volunteer fireman up there, they had a stand pipe and a hose, and that's about all they had, very basic."

Mrs Sylvia Hindmarch still lives in Burnbanks, after moving there with her Burnbanks-born husband, George in 1960. George's parents, George and Olive Hindmarch, came from a farm in Mardale into a new one-bedroomed house in 1931 when his father was employed by the Corporation.

Sylvia's late husband described their house: "This was No 42. It had one bedroom and a living room with an iron stove for heating. The flue pipe went up through the roof. The kitchen had a cast iron bath covered with a wooden top which was used as a table for meals. There were electric lights and also outside a flush toilet with running water. They were called 'honeymoon houses', for young married couples."

George Hindmarch junior as a baby at Burnbanks

After the birth of their two sons (both born in Burnbanks), George and Olive moved into a three-bedroomed house (number 63). Then, because Mr Hindmarch senior kept hens and bees, they eventually moved to number 1 The Oaks where they lived out the rest of their lives.

Sylvia tells us about her in-laws: "George's mum, when she lived across the road there, she still had her old fashioned fire grate you know with the oven on the side which she baked in up till the last. And it used to be baking day on a Wednesday and it was always a sponge cake and a gingerbread and rock buns and scones, once a week! Of course she still had the old set pot boiler which she used to boil the clothes in. Well you fill it full with water and boil the clothes in and keep stoking the fire up underneath with sticks and that. She had an old mangle that she had outside that she used to take the clothes out to mangle (wring) them. Yes it was hard work, yes. George's mum and Mrs Scott next door they used to go sticking into the wood there behind to get the sticks for stoking up the boilers. She did finally get an electric washer in the end but as I say they got by. Of course George's mother was one of these that she wouldn't spend a penny if a ha'penny would do! But of course wages weren't very big in them days and it was how they were brought up.

Folk were friendly in the village as Walter Twigg recalls: "Mrs Jewell - She would have been one of the people, you see there were always women in our house - always full of women chattering ....But the tea was always on."

Burnbanks rules required that you could only keep a dog if you had written permission to do so. Mr Eastham remembers: "We had a dog.....that's one of the things I do remember. They called her Bess. You actually got a certificate I think..... my dad had to get a permit to keep one."

A view over the village rooftops with stove pipes

Hughie Davins and Donald Bird with Glen the dog

MANCHESTER CORPORATION WATERWORKS.

HAWESWATER - SECTION "A".

BURN BANKS VILLAGE.

The Bearer, Charles Eastham being Tenant of No. 30 Hut, has permission to keep 1 Dog until further notice.

It is to be clearly understood that if the Dog is reported, at any time, as being out of control - in any way - it will have to be disposed of.

Engineer - Section "A".

Engineer's Office,
BAMPTON.

16th December 1929.

Mrs Eastham with a dog called Glen, Bobby Eastham, Hughie Davins and Donald Bird

Copy

MANCHESTER CORPORATION WATERWORKS.

HAWESWATER.

MEMORANDUM OF AGREEMENT MADE this ..Sixteenth...... day of .November..... 1929, BETWEEN THE MANCHESTER CORPORATION (hereinafter called "The Corporation") by Lewis Holme Lewis, Engineer and Estate Agent to the Waterworks Committee, of the one part, and ....James Boe........ (hereinafter called the "Tenant") of the other part, WHEREBY THE CORPORATION hereby agrees to let and the tenant agrees to take the ......No. 4 Hut.............. with the appurtenances belonging thereto, situate at Burn Banks Village....... in the parish of .....Bampton.. at a rental of ..Twelve...... shillings ~~and .... pence~~ per week clear of all ....Rates & Taxes....... the tenancy to commence from November 11th 1929 and to be subject to the following conditions :-

1. The rent shall be paid by the tenant on Friday in each week at the Pay Office.
2. The tenancy shall be determined by one week's notice on either side, to be given on any rent day.
3. In case the tenant goes fishing in the lake or in pursuit of rabbits or game, or misconducts himself in any way, or becomes bankrupt, he will be liable to be turned out after one week's notice given by the Engineer.
4. No buildings shall be erected or alterations made in or to the premises by the tenant.
5. The tenant will not be allowed to keep any animals, birds, fowl, or anything living, except with the consent of the Engineer.
6. The tenant shall not cause, permit or suffer any intoxicating liquors to be brought upon the premises in barrels, and shall not sell any intoxicating drinks or provisions therein. In the case of breach of this condition, the tenant will be forthwith ejected.
7. The tenant to purchase food or other things for himself or his lodgers as far as possible at the Canteen or Shops in the Village.
8. If at any time hereafter the tenant shall be discharged from the service of the Corporation, the tenancy shall be forthwith determined.
9. The tenant shall provide for and take lodgers to the number for whom accommodation is available in his hut, and shall at all times endeavour to attend to their reasonable wants and comfort.
10. No lodgers allowed except men who are employed on the Corporation's
11. In case of a lodger desiring to Board and Lodge, the tenant and lodger can arrange reasonable terms, which must be registered at the Office.
12. The tenant shall keep all the glass in the windows and doors and all locks, fastenings and other internal fittings in, upon and belonging to the premises in good and sufficient repair during the tenancy and shall at all times keep the premises in a clean and healthy condition.
13. The tenant shall not leave the premises untenanted or assign or underlet the premises, or use or suffer them to be used in any manner other than as a dwelling house, without the previous consent of the Engineer.
14. The Engineer and anyone authorised by him to be allowed to inspect the premises at any time.
15. No auction sale or sale of any description to take place on the premises without the consent of the Engineer.
16. Any suspicious case of infectious or other disease to be reported at once to the Office on the Works.
17. The greatest care must be taken to prevent any possibility of FIRE. As a rule lights shall be out (except in cubicle alleys) at 11 p.m.
18. In case there shall be a breach of any of the conditions of this Agreement, it shall be lawful for the Corporation to re-enter on the premises and take possession thereof without giving to the tenant any notice to quit, and to eject the tenant therefrom.

IN WITNESS whereof the said LEWIS HOLME LEWIS and the tenant have hereunto set their hands the day and year first hereinbefore written.

Witness to the signature of the said LEWIS HOLME LEWIS

(Signed). L. Holme Lewis.

(Sgd). Albert C. Berry.
Waterworks Offices, Town Hall, Manchester.

Witness to the signature of the said James Boe

(Sgd) James Boe,

4 Burn Banks Village,
(Sgd). P. C. Dickson

Tenancy agreement for one of the boarding houses

The Mission Hall

Practical and spiritual management

A missioner was appointed to care for the souls of the villagers. He lived at the first house in Burnbanks (The Oaks) and had the task of ministering to people of all denominations in the Mission Hall that was in the wood next to his house. To ensure that he visited all the houses he was also made the assistant rent collector.

Next door was the Village Inspector who had to ensure that everything in the village was clean and orderly. The employers were always aware of the danger of the spread of infections with so many people living so close together. To encourage him to keep a check on every house he was also the chief rent collector.

The office where all administration took place was the highest building on the site with a clear view over Burnbanks one way and along the length of the dam in the other direction.

Bill Rawlings tells us about the boss, Mr Jameson: "(*Walmhowe*) That's where Mr Jameson lived. He was a big man - must have been six foot two. And he never used the corporation transport - he had a bike, a great big old bike - it wasn't a penny farthing but it looked a bit like it - and he used to bike up to the offices every day. Very aloof man but he was an engineer. We never spoke to him, we never spoke or anything like that. Oh he was the head engineer, he was the top man of the village, yes."

To maintain law and order PC Ostle (with large Alsatian dog thrown in) was seconded from the County Police force, paid by Manchester and given one of the houses at Burnbanks with a police badge on the door.

Mr Jameson with the vicar of Mardale, the Rev Barham

Mr Eastham explains: "They thought that Burnbanks would be a rough place, and they wanted two or three policemen. But there was only one man there, that was PC Ostle, with a big Alsatian, at number 66."

And Raymond Holliday tells us: "He was greatly feared by all the children, reporting us to our parents for climbing trees, jumping over walls, et cetera – all quite harmless fun!"

PC Ostle and his dog Tarzan outside Burnbanks Police Station

Remembered by many for his strictness, PC Ostle is described here by Bill Rawlings: "Oh yes he was a right character. I think we were all absolutely frightened to death of him. He had his old bike there and he had his Alsatian. My first memory of him, we had a spaniel and it was running among the sheep. I don't think it was worrying them, it was just running among them. Anyway we had it put down, and that's when Dargues had Thornthwaite Hall - or should I say 'Thornthet'. He virtually forced them to have it put down. He was very good at taking licences out, going round the farms and seeing if the sheep were dipped and all the illegal slaughtering of pigs which went on during the war – everybody knows that. He'd always get his share in of course, like all of us."

Walter Twigg, Bill Rawling's half-brother, was one of twin boys born at Burnbanks in 1936 to Bill's mother, Jessie, after she married Mr Bill Twigg. He has vivid memories of PC Ostle: "We seemed to be always in mischief, that seemed to be a regular occurrence for me and the boys – me and Tom, my twin brother and another lad called Alan Malpass. There was a policeman, PC Ostle, I think they called him, he just seemed to have a downer on us and didn't leave us alone – but we had fun."

He also remembers PC Ostle giving boys a ticking off for swinging on the big long gate at the entrance to the village, at Naddlegate. The late George Hindmarch also talked of a gate at the entrance to the village, which he recalls being locked and no-one being allowed in without permission. Meanwhile Tom Moore recalls that PC Ostle carved a deer out of wood and kept it for some years on display in his garden.

Arthur Cannon, who lived at the village club, explains that PC Ostle possibly resented the fact that he wasn't supposed to go into the club unless in a professional capacity: "He used to come round and knock at the door, then have me outside

Twins Walter and Tommy Twigg with Mrs Pugh

looking to see that there was a chink of light showing in the window that wasn't right and should be covered up. That was one of his duties. He didn't really care for the Cannon family because Colin hadn't been there too long when he got a knock at the door and he introduced himself as the village constable: 'Everything all right, Mr Cannon?' and Colin said yes, everything was, and he hung about a lot and anyway he did eventually go. Colin always said he thought he was after a drink so he never gave him one. See, he wasn't allowed to enter those club premises unless he was required, so to get a drink he had to go all the way to the Haweswater Hotel."

Chris Holme (b 1941) lived at Bampton and went to school with about 15 Burnbanks children. He recalls: "And probably the other reason we didn't go up there was because there was a policeman there and we were always terrified of the policeman. Every now and again he would pay a visit down to Bampton, probably once a week, and always unexpected, to see what we were up to down here. And honestly, just the appearance of the policeman coming down on his bicycle to see if we were behaving ourselves was enough to keep us all in line in them days. So we had great respect for the policeman really."

Records show that there were other policemen after PC Ostle moved away. One may have been called Towns or Tamms and another, according to George Brunskill who lived at Naddle at the time, was Norman Kendall.

George told us: "He was a good policeman. If there were troublemakers he'd pick them up by the back of the neck and chuck them over the fence. He could keep order! After him we didn't have a policeman but Sgt Ivinson came down from Shap. He would give us a kick if we were misbehaving!"

But none crop up in recollections quite like PC Ostle. George even remembers his Morris car number US 9010, and that he wore his full uniform when riding around on his bicycle. This newspaper report on the right appeared in The Herald in May 1939.

A medical centre was provided at the back of the village with a village nurse and Dr Prentice used to come from Shap. Bobby Eastham remembers: "Dr Prentice, used to come from Shap, as far as I know he used to come every Saturday and it was up the back road, there was like a little place

MAY 13, 1939.

NEXT week the Corporation of Manchester will make an official inspection of the Haweswater dam which, it is expected, will be completed before the autumn of next year. It is rather an imposing spectacle in concrete at the moment, but this and the fact that it will make a very good air-raid shelter in the event of a war is referred to in an article on another page. What I wish to say here is that the Corporation might make an inspection of the village gardens, and if they do they would have to award first prize to the garden of the village policeman, which is the first to be seen at the entrance to the village. The garden is embellished with bird baths and bird tables in the shape of pigeon cotes and these stand in blazing beds of scarlet saxifrage (known to nurserymen as Bathoniensis) while other rock plants like purple aubretia make up a carpet and a carnival of colour. Here is one policeman who is making the world a little gayer than he found it, but whether his wife mows the lawn as well as answers the telephone and collects the sheep-dip papers I do not know. They at least set an example to their neighbours in the way of garden adornment which will not be without effect in a community which may be here to-day and gone to-morrow. Burn Banks is a well-behaved village and this may give the policeman more time to cultivate mignonette instead of devoting the whole of it to the correction of morals. At any rate a garden is a lovesome thing, God wot, and a policeman perspiring over perennials is a more elevating sight than a policeman shouldering a noisy navvy as a casualty along the Via Dolorosa to Shap Police Station. Not that any of the skilled workers at Burn Banks would put him to so much trouble. They would rather give him a hand with his garden or follow his example by breaking up a bit of fell prairie and make one of their own. There is nothing so civilising as a garden, especially in a district where every prospect pleases and man is far from vile.

SILVERPEN.

where you used to go. And then they had a nurse, there was always a village nurse. If you went to Dr Prentice it was nearly always iodine."

Tom Moore tells us that the nurse was called McCormick, from Bampton Grange and that Manchester Corporation kept an ambulance on the dam in case of an emergency. Some people recall being given a lift to school in the ambulance. Mrs Sharp remembers an accident while the village children were playing in the water: "Betty Thompson was climbing up the fall rocks (daredevil) and an eel slithered out from under her foot and it cut an artery. She bled dreadfully and had to be taken away in the village ambulance, all bandaged."

The minute book of Manchester Corporation Waterworks Committee records that in September 1935, Mr G Slade, who was employed as a chainman, had suffered a 'paralytic stroke' and was not fit enough to resume duties. The Waterworks Committee agreed to pay for his belongings to be taken back to Birmingham. But it was decided that since his illness had apparently not been caused by his work, the Committee was not liable. As Mr and Mrs Slade were in 'very necessitous circumstances' a compassionate grant of £10 was made.

The minutes also record that there were seven accidents in 1928 and 21 in 1929 on the Haweswater Aqueduct. £84.10s.1d compensation had been paid in total.

The doctor, however, was not always the best person to treat a patient it seems. Maighread Sharp's mother had a lot of trouble in her pregnancy. She was anaemic and exhausted, her daughter recalls: "Then she got a very bad infection in her left hand which became painful and swollen. After nearly a week of pain she went to the doctor in Penrith and he lanced the centre of it in the shape of a cross. It was easy for a day or two but grew bad again. But it was the kindness and helpful work of a friendly next door neighbour who (*helped most by*) putting red hot poultices on the wound four times a day until the poison all came away. This was Mrs. Duncan who lived at No 6. She was an easy-going woman who swore like a navvie but could tuck a baby under her arm while stirring the dinner with the other arm and then turn round and smack her little boy Angus away from the biscuits on the table while laughing about a silly joke. Her house was untidy most of the time but her kind heart and unceasing devotion certainly saved the situation."

Ernest Martin at No 39 Burnbanks. The doctor's surgery is on the right of the picture.

Chris Holme's father, Harry, who provided the local bus service, contracted tuberculosis in his younger days. Chris explains his treatment: "(*They*) used to think only cure for TB was fresh air. They didn't go to the sanatorium. They had a shed up back of the mill there. There's a little hill up there called Pocket Money Hill they call it – I don't know how it gets that name – and dad had a shed there and he lived in that shed for about six months

An old tin shed and that was to try and get over his TB."

Joyce Arran lived at a house close to the doctor's surgery and she remembers playing there. Her mother was apparently employed to keep the surgery clean.

"We thought it was great because we could play in there, jumping on that bed that the doctor had there. There was just a bed. There wasn't drugs or anything like - not that I remember. No, it was just a desk and chairs and then there was this bed but it was on wheels which gave us great thrills, (*we*) pushed it about…"

Babies were mostly delivered at home. The fact that the first baby born in Burnbanks was named Irene Burnbanks Thompson would suggest a level of affection which the residents felt for their village.

A Trio of Twins.

THREE PROUD MOTHERS AT BURN BANKS, HAWESWATER.

THE picture shows three sets of twins with their mothers at the Burn Banks Clinic, run by the Westmorland County Council. The children are John and Maureen Clark, son and daughter of Mr. and Mrs. J. Clark; John and Walter Twigg, sons of Mr. and Mrs. W. Twigg; and David and Douglas McColl, sons of Mr. and Mrs. W. McColl. The fathers work on the Manchester Corporation Waterworks.

Photo: Frank Kenyon, Penrith.

Three sets of Burnbanks twins with their mother. Thomas and Walter Twigg with their mother Jessie, John and Maureen Clark with Mrs J Clark, and David and Douglas MacColl with mother Muriel. (The Herald, August 28th 1937)

Rum Butter

Melt 1lb butter, add 11/2 lbs brown sugar, 2 teaspoons grated nutmeg. Mix well and add and 1 wineglass of rum then beat until it starts to thicken. Pour into a bowl and leave to set.

This recipe was apparently associated with childbirth. It was kept in a special dish, often a family heirloom and partaken of by all who visited the new arrival. It was eaten with thin oatcakes. Superstition has it that the woman who first cuts into the bowl will be the next to have need of a similar dish on her own account! Formerly it was a custom to hide the bowl and for young boys to search for it, then after eating its contents the bowl would be passed round for a collection, the proceeds being laid by for the benefit of the new baby.

From a recipe given to Margaret Edkins by Dr Judson's wife.

Mothers and children at the Burnbanks clinic in about 1937. The lady behind the two mothers with babies on their laps is Mrs Muriel MacColl with twins David and Douglas, Mrs Twigg and her son Brian, 3rd on back row with no hat, Mrs C Malpas with son John in front of Mrs Twigg and Mrs Holliday with Raymond, wearing a hat with a flower on the 3rd row from the back with Mrs Crabtree to their left.

The caption reads: The Westmorland County Council holds a Maternity and Child Welfare Clinic at Burn Banks, Haweswater, every month the great majority of the mothers being wives of workers on the Manchester Corporation Waterworks at Haweswater. A voluntary committee of which Mrs W H M Jameson is the secretary, is responsible for the clinic, which is in charge of Dr J Wright, Assistant County Medical Officer. Nurse McCormick, Bampton, is in attendance...

A job to be done

They came with a stick over their shoulder with a red handkerchief and that was all their belongings in there ....Some started at 7.30am and were sacked by 12 noon. Mr Jameson was the resident engineer and every afternoon did a tour of the site works, the offices being located on the hillside. They were very hard on them (the navvies), the foremen, you know, he'd be stood there all weather watching them and he'd have a dewdrop from his nose, he wouldn't wipe it – but he was more interested in what they were doing. Oh yes, it was hard.

Arthur Cannon

It had been hoped that at a time of serious unemployment everywhere, the local community would benefit from the provision of jobs at Burnbanks and some local men were eventually employed on building the new road along the hillside to the east and above the lake which was to replace the old road on the west of the lake through Mardale which would soon be flooded. Penrith Urban District Council wrote to the Manchester Corporation Waterworks Committee in January 1930 asking for local men to be employed: 'Locally a good type of man for such work as you have now in progress is available, and facilities for journeys to and from the works by bus can be put into operation.'

It is also recorded in Bampton Parish Council minutes in December 1934 that the Clerk was asked to write to Mr Jameson asking him to forward to Manchester Waterworks Committee a request to 'consider kindly an application for work made by unemployed residents in Bampton'.

The minutes of the Westmorland County Council's Main Roads Committee, apparently recorded that: 'The Manchester Corporation had in contemplation the immediate starting of certain roads, particularly the one from Shap Station and one higher up the valley, and that they would introduce into the county 100 or 150 of the unemployed with a grant from the Ministry of Labour. The roads would take two or three years, and by that time it was anticipated that the other works would start and employment would then be found for 10 or 12 years.'

The new road to Mardale to the east of the lake was a major project involving explosives as it was being cut out of the steep hillside high above the lake and it was hoped that later it would become a tourist attraction. When eventually it was completed the Waterworks Committee considered the possibility of making it a toll road, with tourists paying to drive to the end of the valley to enjoy the impressive mountain scenery surrounding the new lake. But the industrial mess which surrounded the building of the dam would have provided a disincentive to tourism.

When the houses were completed the construction of the dam began. In 1935 the foundation stone for the dam was laid by Alderman William Walker.

Work on the dam in Autumn 1939

A view of the dam works with the blondins

A group of labourers, Gerry Dawson second from the left

Alderman William Walker laying the foundation stone of the dam, 1935. Taken from the Manchester Guardian

Navvies mixing concrete

The late George Hindmarch told us about the building work: "The work would likely be colossal to what they'd been used to if they'd come out of a factory. They were out here in rain and muck and puddle. They didn't stop long, like. Arthur Robinson, Neville's dad, he was a tailor and come up here to picks and shovels. But Arthur, he stopped, like."

John Graham, now living in Shap, used to visit Burnbanks as a lad when he was employed as a van boy by a general merchant in Shap. He tells us: "Well, working conditions in those days were vastly different to what we have now. I mean, the pictures of the workmen working there, they had hardly any protective clothing for a start off, no hard hats and all that kind of thing which goes hand in glove nowadays. And as far as strikes I don't think there was actually a strike as such. (*But one was*) threatened because the rate of pay was just 11½d an hour. And working knee deep in concrete was a very arduous job. And (*they*) threatened a strike to get better working conditions, and they were eventually awarded 3d an hour. Which brought their pay up to something in the region of 1s 2½d an hour or to bring it back to today's terms round about £2.15 for a 45 hour week. Which, you know, I can't even get a pint of Guinness for that now, never mind a week's work. And therefore, at one period of time as well, I understand at the start of the project that workmen didn't get what they called wet pay, if they were rained off well that was it they just had lost their pay, but I think that was righted eventually as far as I understand."

"It was manual labour you know. They didn't have the machinery. When you see photographs of the dam being built I mean, by today's standards it's very archaic indeed. I mean as I've just mentioned, men working knee deep in concrete with no protective clothing, you know and so, I would think, well I think 75% of the work would be all manual labour."

One young Burnbanks worker lost his life in a tragic accident in 1932. George Hindmarch described this event, having heard tell of it as a boy and still having a copy of the cutting from the newspaper at the time. The boy and his family all lived at Burnbanks: "One brother was just finishing his shift and his brother about to take over and there was an explosion. The brother going in was the one that brought him out."

The boy died later of his injuries and his father apparently tried unsuccessfully to get compensation from the employers. The 19 year-old boy, Frederick Kyle's grave is in Bampton Cemetery with a tombstone dated 1932. It reads:

The blow was great
The shock severe
We never thought the end so near

1932 8—THE HERALD, SATURDAY, NOVEMBER 2

DEATH FOLLOWS MARDALE EXPLOSION.

An Injured Man Dies in Infirmary.

CHANGED PLACES WITH FELLOW-WORKER WHO WAS UNHURT.

Working on building the dam

Some of the workers

Above the dam site, running right across the valley, was an overhead cable line which allowed heavy materials and containers of wet concrete to be deposited exactly where they were needed. It was powered by electricity provided by a diesel generator in a quarry on the Naddle side of the valley. The system had been constructed by a firm from Aberdeen. There are still people living in the Penrith area who came from Aberdeen to work on this overhead cable line.

Bill Rawlings describes the electricity supply at Burnbanks: "If you ever walk along the east side of the lake you'll see a wire now and again going along it well they used to take the electricity right up the east side and it went across just by the narrows and up into the Haweswater Hotel, so the Haweswater hotel had electricity right from the word go….it was a generator. I can't say whether it was oil or solid fuel - I can't remember that. But Harry Toone he worked there as a boiler man and they used to charge all the village batteries, the accumulators, anybody that could afford a wireless had them but they were run off wet batteries, the accumulators, and they used to charge them there, oh, maybe for a penny or tuppence or something like that."

Bill Toone and a colleague preparing wood for dam-building

Tom Moore's father worked shifts in the power station. He recalls that the electricity plant was shut down at about 11pm for the night. Mrs Sharp also recalls that Mr Ord was in charge of the power station.

Raymond Holliday's father had come to Burnbanks in 1925, before the village was built. He had already worked for Manchester Corporation Water Works at Thirlmere. Initially he had lodgings at Dennyhill then, after getting married, moved into rooms at Eastward with Mr and Mrs Thompson whose family still farm there. His father's job at first was maintaining the farms which the Corporation had acquired around the valley and fellsides. Then, when the actual dam project began, he was a ganger on the building of the new road from Burnbanks up to Mardale. We have already heard how Mrs Sharp (MacColl)'s father was desperate and weary when he made his way over the fells from Longsleddale to Burnbanks to seek employment. He too had to take unskilled work until a job came up in the power station to suit his experience.

Arthur Cannon arrived in Burnbanks to live with his brother and sisters who were running the club. He had lost both parents and spent his childhood on his uncle's farm at Stainmore after the death of his parents, being the youngest of five. He was just 14 when he began work as an electrician in 1937. He admits that his memories of Burnbanks are almost 70 years-old and may not be correct in every detail but he goes on to tell us: "I commenced work in short trousers but later had long bib and brace overalls. Fred Bourne was the foreman electrician and, if I remember correctly, there were two other electricians and one mate. Frank Millican was one of the electricians and Harry Toone was the mate. I was like the apprentice.

"(*The building we worked in*) was of wooden construction with an iron stove and my first job was to light the stove, make the tea. You had the usual tricks played on you as a young boy. Probably such as when working for Frank Millican in the dam and he'd say, 'Look, we're trying to reach up to something we can't get to. Just pop along to the electricians' shop and see Tommy Wilson, see if you can get the long stand off him'. So you went for the long stand and that's all you got – it was a long stand: 'Wait over there!'

"There were about four other staff and you were sent with them and you watched what they did. I must have had a good knowledge of what they did because you were able to repair cables on your own at a very young age. We carried out all the electrical work in the course of construction of the dam and I also remember assisting to lay the 3.5 KV cable which runs from the dam and terminates in the substation located in the garage at the foot of the hotel. The cable runs behind the wall on the main road to the Haweswater hotel. Power lines and telephone lines were run round the village, which covered some 60 buildings, for the navvies and work people and probably a dozen or so staff bungalows for senior people.

Work in progress

"In the village substation I carried out the work of charging batteries for the radio sets. DC power was supplied by two Rushton Hornsby generating sets with a further one I believe on standby and there was also an AC rotary converter coupled to them.

"Hours of work were 49½ a week from 7.30am to 5pm Monday to Friday with a half hour lunch break. Saturdays were 7.30am to 12 noon. Every six months on a Saturday you were sacked to avoid paying superannuation as the work was only classed as temporary. You clocked on and off each day eyed closely by one-eyed "Hock-eye" Johnson to ensure you clocked no one else in.

".. it was only by having seen what was done that you were able to do this work. The others were senior to me – they were in their twenties and they would serve their apprenticeships with local electrical contractors such as, say, WH Smith of Penrith. While I was there, I think he was the man who opened the dam, Alderman Sir William Walker, he came to reside in one of the staff bungalows at the village and I remember being sent down there and doing some additional wiring in that bungalow for him. He wanted sockets, electric clock points and lights in different places."

The big dig

Some workers building the dam

A trio of workmates on the dam

Mr Cannon explains how difficult some of the work was: "As the dam got up (*to full height*) – well the length of it is roughly quarter of a mile and it's roughly 100 foot high where the slipway is - I had some arduous tasks. I used to have to go up into the control room at one side, climb up the steps and carry out maintenance work on the machinery within the tower that drove the cableway across the dam. I had to do work up at the valve shaft – that's about a mile beyond the Haweswater Hotel.

"That's where the water is taken through the fellside to the north side of Kendal, tunnelled through. I think that was tunnelled before the actual work commenced on the building of the dam in 1930 – I think that was done in the 1920s. There could have been one or two people killed when that tunnel was built. And from there there's a joining point with the Thirlmere one and it's taken through. There's booster pumps on the way through. I did the electrical work installing the pumps in the bottom of the valve shaft.

"It was marvellous to see the dam being constructed as it went up, you know shuttering work. Then where the concrete mixing was and then the skip overhead, came down and picked the skip up full of concrete and then they were taken up and then there would be a flagman waving it through, Jack Fountain would be in the control tower, it would come forward then let it down. And it wasn't just done in nice fine weather, it was sometimes torrential rain.

"When the dam was first electrified I had the job – there were no power tools. Well, there'd be a dozen conduits going east, a dozen conduits going west along the chambers inside the dam and these conduits, metal pipes, were supported on brackets and you had to fasten those brackets to the concrete wall of the dam and you did that by hammer and chisel, there was no simple thing like a power tool to drill a hole to put a rawl plug in. And the number of times you missed the tool and hit your hand. It wasn't very nice really. There was one thing about it really: it was good if it was winter time because it was warm in there. But summer time it was absolutely freezing, but winter time you could feel the heat as you walked in. You could walk right through from one end to the other. Now, that was done with conduits and what they called VIR cables but unfortunately due to the condensation in the dam with this type of wiring the conduits got full of water so there was faults developing greatly so the whole thing had to be redone. It was redone after my time there, it was redone with pyrotechnics cabling which is a solid cable not affected by dampness, but these before were like

INTERIOR OF THE HAWESWATER DAM.

MANY people, when looking at the concrete dam growing at the foot of Haweswater are unaware that it is anything but solid. Inside the Pyramid are a long series of huge concrete chambers, and these are shown in the picture.

The dam interior 1938 from an article in an unidentified newspaper

pipes with cable running through them so naturally there was junction boxes and so forth. You couldn't stop condensation getting in them.

"I got 8/6 a week when I went into the electricians' shop - that was my pay. Well, you were better paid if you got a job as, I think it was called, a 'nipper', getting tea for a few of the navvies. You got sixpence a man off the navvy if you brewed tea for him. So you only needed maybe half a dozen of those and you were better off in pay (than me) and as a young lad I used to think I'd be better off than chipping flipping holes in the concrete to put these cables on.

"(*The navvies*) they didn't stop. And I think these boys, they must have been employed by the corporation to do that, or whether you just went on to the site and you were allowed to do that and collect this money. But you certainly did get fallouts between the boys because you'd probably pinched one of his customers.

"Also, round there while the dam was being constructed there was this miniature railway line. Well, that was quite an attraction. They'd say, 'Oh hello Arthur!' and they were riding round on it and you'd think, 'I would sooner have that job than the job I've got,' little realising that at the end of the day there was nothing for you. See, I was fortunate that my brother Colin was able to get me the job in there."

Arthur also remembers others who worked at Burnbanks: "Albert Ord was in charge of the diesel generating plant and the Jewells were members of his staff. Sid Wear was in charge of building maintenance, Bill Pugh the joiners' shop. Tommy Wilson was a joiner and also Walter Bracken who came on his motor bike from Penrith each day. Alec Little was a blacksmith from Bomby. Alf Mounsey from Bampton was employed as a lorry driver and Jack Hutchinson from Bampton Grange as a dry-stone-waller. Bill Sandham was painter/decorator and sign-writer. Harry Dodd was chief sawyer. Harry Eastham and his son Bobby were office staff. Jack Fountain and his sons were employed on the cableway which ran above the dam to carry the skips of concrete required in the construction. Bill Kirby was a flagman employed on this work."

Workers next to the railway

Marjorie Ord wrote to us telling us about her father's work at Burnbanks, firstly as an employee of Ruston and Hornby Ltd, who were a firm of engineers supplying and maintaining oil generators. He was responsible in 1930 for installing the engines in the generating station and was then kept on by Manchester Corporation Water Works to maintain the power station. They were the original occupants of Number 2 Naddlegate where they lived until Mr Ord returned to Manchester in 1943.

Albert Ord (left) with colleagues

A newspaper photograph (publication unknown) of Robert John Holme

Mr Robert Holme, Chris Holme's grandfather, played an important role at the outset of the dam project. In 1954 the Cumberland and Westmorland Herald carried an article about him celebrating his 92nd birthday and on his 88th birthday in 1950 the same newspaper had carried this article:

In this scheme Mr Robert John Holme played a vital and difficult part in the early stages.

The engineers who were to drive a tunnel from the head of the Haweswater Valley to Longsleddale through which the water was to flow on its way to Manchester, wanted ten foot high observation piers built on the summit of four crags – Lad Cragg, Mardale Banks, Artle Cragg and Swindale Head at the top end of the valley. These were needed for accurate surveying.

The hazardous job of carrying stone, cement and water to these craggy summits – one is over 2,000 feet high – was left to Mr Holme, who was then over 60, and Mr B Martin also of Bampton.

Never had Mr Holme tackled such a difficult job. He found that his two mares were not capable of struggling up the scree-covered gills. Only a spirited Clydesdale stallion could manage to climb the slopes, and when it set off on a wild scramble it was impossible to walk beside it. Mr Holme had quite often to unharness it in one of its struggles.

Chris Holme tells us about his grandfather: "Grandad, he was on contract work for the old Manchester Corporation with his horse and cart, and he got the job of carting the material up to the sighting blocks for the line of the tunnel that goes from the draw-off tower through to Longsleddale. If you look up on top of Lad Crag which is just at the back of Measand, there's a big cairn there and that is a sighting block for the line of the tunnel. The next one is Sleddale Pike or something, right above Mosedale Cottage. There's one on the top of there. Now that is the exact line of the tunnel that goes through. And he got the job of carting all the cement and materials required to build these cairns up there. The cairns were to mark where the tunnel would go. He used to tell me that his old horses weren't strong enough so he had to buy a big strong stallion horse to get the stuff up there. So he had some fond memories of carting stuff up there. He just did one trip a day and that was enough for the horse obviously."

Mr Holme and his stallion

Mr Holme aged 92, still wearing clogs

Surveying on the fell

Breaking stone (one of these men could be Victor Slessor)

Chris also explains where the stone came from during the road and dam building: "There was a big quarry there just below Walla Crag. When the water's up you can't see it but when there's low level you can see where the quarry is then in the reservoir. It would be crushed on site and used as the bigger aggregate for building the dam and then the walls up the sides I think there was big crushers on the sides of the road when they built the new road – you know there wasn't a road on the left hand side of the lake before it started. Jack Hutchinson – people who've heard of Ada Preston – her dad - would be in charge of all that lot. He was the foreman on that stretch up there and it's built absolutely perfect is that wall all the way up there. It's absolutely marvellous it really is. It's a marvellous piece of engineering on its own without the dam."

Mrs June Nanson, Mr Holliday's sister, tells us about her father's work: "My dad used to go round the farms doing maintenance work for various reasons and he got interested in clocks and watches. He became quite an accomplished clock repairer and we got to know loads of people on the farms roundabout after he'd been visiting them, in his own time of course, and he used to come home with things like farm butter and fresh eggs and if they'd had a pig killing day he'd come home with sausages and bacon and all sorts of things and that was absolutely super. I remember that specially. He always had an interest in watch and clock repairing even after he retired."

Sylvia Hindmarch's father-in-law used to work the horses for his brother-in-law when they were building the road and he was also a rock driller and then later employed on maintenance.

Mrs Joyce Aran's father, Ernest Martin, also worked on maintenance and his father, Benjamin Martin, was in charge of the gang of maintenance workers. They moved to Burnbanks in about 1931 when Mrs Aran recalls there was a shortage of work and people coming from all over to seek employment.

Bobby Eastham's father worked in the joinery department: "The dam was made of concrete obviously, and the shuttering was put up for the concrete, and he was responsible for all the bolts that held that shuttering and he had to make sure all the nuts and bolts were oiled and greased so that they could be taken out and used again."

Mr Eastham also recalls his own first pay packet: "I worked at Burnbanks in the stores department where they distributed materials. I would be about 15, I would think. And it was sixteen and fourpence, and the fourpence would just buy a Mars bar. I always bought my mother a Mars bar every week."

Bill Rawlings saw the dam "right from its rock - right till it finished." In his interview he says: "(*They*) always fascinated me - the wagons coming down the concrete road with the cement and whatever it was and bringing it down. And there was a very big mixer. They used to put it in that, mix it all up. And then there was the blondin that went right across the valley. It was a two wire blondin, one bucket would go across and back again like this, take it to (where) the joiners would all shutter up, get all the wooden shuttering up, and then they'd pour the concrete that had been mixed at the other end. And then the navvies would get in where the shuttering

Cableway across the valley with the site for the Dam cleared below- shortly after work restarted in 1934.

was, tip the concrete and pull it out with their shovels. They had big thigh boots on, hobnails on the bottom, and they would paddle among it. And they had a compressor, a big compressor with vibrators on and they just would be going round with these vibrators, paddling all the time in it.

"Then of course the blondin worked the whole time of the dam. Up and down and across. And when it got to where you wanted to tip it it'd come right down and they'd tip it as I say and paddle it in and use the vibrators. It would go back up again and back to be loaded up. This was going on all the time. Well there was a man, like the ski lift now, he was on the controls. He used to send them across and they would go round and come back again. Done with a motor and there was someone controlling it."

Walter Twigg describes his father's job as a labourer: "I think he used to work what they'd call a blondin, like a big wire from one side of the valley to the other, just with a swing thing carrying concrete … working from one side to the other, and mix concrete in it and tip it. He was just sitting in there operating that and apart from that he was just an ordinary labourer. And he did work on the new road building the walls; I know he built. He was also labouring for the man who built the three tier garage up at Haweswater Hotel, it's still there actually. And he used to walk up the fells reading rain gauges, that was maybe two days a week he'd be doing that job. Oh it'd be a wet job many times but they had to be read like. He'd be on top of Walla Crag and then on the other side but there was no doubt he'd have loved that job. He was always a man with dogs anyway."

Subsequent to a Mardale exhibition in 1995 at Shap, Mr Delwyn Davies, living in Cheshire, wrote to the organisers. He had visited and become very fond of the Haweswater valley as a teenager. He even stayed at Measand Beck Farm at one point and remembers hearing of the plans for a dam. He wrote: "About a decade later I found myself (*employed as*) a civil engineer with a lovely new wife living at Naddle Gate on the dam. Seventh heaven it was.

"On the dam we had three well-behaved groups of men. The regular navvies who moved from project to project; the casuals, mostly from West Cumberland, and the ticket-of-leave men who reported to the police weekly at the bottom of the resident engineer's garden.

Excavations at the Haweswater dam site

"Soldier Burns (who was not unlike 'Lordy' (*presumably Lord Lonsdale - known as the Yellow Earl*) relatively wealthy with his army pension would stand proudly in the square at Penrith on a Saturday afternoon in his new brown corduroy suit – his waistcoat with six pockets, his jacket with more, his trousers neatly tied with cord below the knee, and a red handkerchief round his throat, all surmounted by a hard bowler hat to announce his social seniority.

"Another man, as poor as a church mouse invented the birth of nations: not satisfied with the annual gift of a child, they produced one very nine months. Their furniture almost wholly of 'Maypole' margarine boxes. The family were 13 in number when I last saw them.

"During the lunch break the men competed in carrying the blacksmith's anvil, the small 50lb one, up the 90 foot ladder of the blondin tower, walked across the 12 foot plank to descend the twin ladder of blondin 2. The game was stopped before someone fell off.

"There were bad accidents with several men killed in the Mardale tunnel. And the Naddle Forest midges played havoc with some men.

"I recall 'Watery Willie' who read the rain gauges so meticulously. He came from Shap, and was also the country postman. And Dr Prentice of Shap, a nice man - he always seems to arrive when I had recovered."

Mr Davies also sheds light on how the blondins got their name: "Blondin towers carried the cableways across the valley – the cables being called after the high wire walker."

In fact the Frenchman Jean Blondin (1824-1897), was famous for his high-wire crossings of the Niagara Falls. This system of cables became known as 'blondins' and was also used when building the Churchill Barriers off Orkney during the war.

Margaret Higson remembers visiting her father who was an engineering draghtsman, in his office next to The Oaks: "(*It* was) a room at the end of a long building where Mr Harry Walker had his tools for his work – mole traps I can remember. In dad's office there were always drawings on his desk of buildings belonging to Burnbanks – he was an excellent draughtsman and neat writer."

Tommy Toone, was a blacksmith's striker. Bill Rawling tells us about his work: "Built like a brick. And he worked all the way through from when it started up again. Well, in those days they were nearly all navvies, no JCBs, picks and shovels. They had to make their own picks and sharpen the picks, sharpen the shovels, do all this. Well the blacksmith, he would get his tongs, put his red hot iron on the (*anvil*) the blacksmith's striker fired it up, the blacksmith got his tongs, held it there and told the striker where to hit, you know he put his thing there and the striker hit it, to sharpen them up. So the blacksmith actually was doing the job but he was the man with a hammer hitting it.

"As I say Tommy Toone was a blacksmith's striker, right through to definitely 1939-40. The dam was about finished then and they started making perch traps for putting in the lake to catch perch for the war effort to send through to a factory in Leeds.

"When it was filling up they were putting these perch traps in with a rope on and a glass ball - I've still got a glass ball. And then when it rained it came up that fast that it left quite a lot of them down below. There'll be some in the bottom there now. I can say as well years and years later when the level dropped we did get one perch trap out still, no perch in but there was trout in so the trout must have been living on other things coming in, and there was just this one trout in. That's just one recollection I've got of that episode."

Bill Rawling's first job at the age of about 15 was doing forestry work at Chapel Hill, Mardale: "I started (*forestry*) with Jim Jeffries as his mate on a wagon. I went to Penrith and had an interview to be a motor mechanic at Tinkler's and the wage was going to be 12/6 a week and my bus fare was going to be - no, my wage was going to be 7/6 a week and my bus fare was going to be 12/6. I was going to lose money going and I couldn't pay that, I wanted some pocket money so I had an interview and started in the works at a pound a week and that was Monday till Saturday afternoon.

"...looking across down to the old Dun Bull, I planted 75 percent of those trees. I planted Norwegian spruce, larch, a few Sitka, and - which you won't see now, because they'd miscalculated, all the hard woods were all washed out, all beech, sycamore, oak. They were lower down and the lake come up unfortunately too high and took them all away. I think the Friends of the Lake District said they had to have hard woods as well. So we had

Burnbanks blacksmith shop. Left to right: A Little, W Holliday, unknown

four - one, two, three, four rows of hard woods and then the soft woods behind that. The soft woods would go as pit props because I only planted them five foot apart.

"I had to make a cut like the shape of a T with a spade, lifted it up and pushed your tree in and your trees were only about nine inches to a foot. Then just put your heel in and that was it then got the next one.

"When people were going away from the allotments then we commandeered about the first, from the works side, about four allotments and we grew our own spruce - Norwegian spruce,

Sitka spruce, Japanese larch, I don't think we planted any larch, it was always Japanese larch because it's a very fast grower.

"The forester then was Jim Jeffries and he lived at Helton and he used to come up. He also had two works wagons. Jim was one and Arthur Robinson was the driver of the other one. Now Arthur, he used to take the men over to Garnet Bridge every day, that's the straining wells, every morning he took a load over in his wagon then brought them back and that was about the last project to go ahead. Now the other wagon - as I say I worked with Jim and we used to - we were on the forestry but we also went round the farms if they wanted timber, things like that, we would take that up and drop that and come back. Then he'd leave me planting trees and he would go down to Penrith during the war and pick up the lobster and stuff for the hotel, for the councillors and the big boys coming up. People from Manchester, yes, Manchester Corporation, town councillors whatever they call themselves. Oh they lived - there was good meals up there."

In about 1940 Tom Moore got a job in the fitting shop: "I was more or less a tea boy. I was on that for about six months till it closed down, then I was put on the wagon as a second man, with Arthur Robinson for about 18 months. Then I left there in 1942 to serve my time as a fitter at Altham's in Penrith."

Most women in those days stayed at home as 'housewives'. Mrs Nanson tells us about her mother: "Mum was a housewife of course. Not many women went out to work in those days - except when Dad was called up in the army during the last war Mum had to go out to work because the army pay was so poor. She worked in Penrith for a while. (*And*) she worked for Mrs Forge at Walm Howe. I remember I used to cycle down with loads of freshly ironed sheets on the bike down to Walm Howe. And then eventually she got a job at the school canteen with Ada Preston as cook and worked there for I think 25 years all told and became cook-in-charge when Ada Preston retired. She cycled daily to Bampton School from Burnbanks in all kinds of weather - four miles in total. She loved her work there making excellent meals (I still get good reports from ex-pupils!)."

Bill Twigg (left), Walter's father, who worked as a labourer on the dam, with three colleagues

Recession halts works

Almost as soon as work began it was disrupted and progress threatened by an industrial dispute when the management proposed that though all workers would be paid at the same rate, those on the government's subsidised scheme would not have paid holidays while those who had been directly recruited by Manchester would. This may have resulted from an urgent need to save money. In 1930 wages were reduced by ½d per hour and, in 1932, all work on the dam ceased due to the effects on Manchester of a world-wide recession.

WAGES AT HAWESWATER.

Men Apply for Increased Pay.

The Manchester Corporation Waterworks Committee, it is announced, has received an application for an increase in wages from the men employed on their Haweswater scheme, and the matter has been referred for consideration to a special sub-committee.

Some 200 men are at present employed on the Haweswater scheme, but this number will shortly be increased by some thousands. The men are asking for an increase which will bring their rate of pay to 1s. 2½d. per hour. At present, under the provisions of the Civil Engineers' Conciliation Board agreement, they are receiving 11½d. per hour, which does not enable them, working full time, to earn £2 10s. a week, and out of this they pay 25s. a week for board and lodging. It is also pointed out that they receive nothing for "wet time," and as the district is one of the wettest in the country the point is considered one of considerable importance.

A cutting from an unknown newspaper about the wage dispute

The families remained at Burnbanks but many of the men, single men in particular, found themselves without work and went off to look for work in other parts of the country. Some men were given work on the tunnel through the mountain between Mardale and Long Sleddale, which was the section of the pipeline to Manchester on which work continued. Other men were given work at the rate of one week in every three in Burnbanks on general cleaning and maintenance. It was a very worrying time.

Bill Rawlings remembers his mother's brother having to leave home: "Now then, the depression came just about that time and Bill lost his job on the tunnel and I don't think Harry had started working then so there was something about the means test that Bill had to leave home, something like that, so where he went and how he - whether they slept in tents. But certain ones had to leave the houses."

Walter Twigg remembers: "When the works closed down for a couple of years, mother and father (*Bill Twigg*) went back to where he used to live. That must have been before they got Number 5; and that was where their first son was born in Great Broughton, Salford. Then the job opened up again and they came back and they must have got this house."

Bobby Eastham recalls how they, as a family, were able to remain at Burnbanks: "When my father was out of work, when the dam was stopped for two years and four months, he worked one week in three, then. In the week that they did work, they had to do everything, they couldn't just pick their job They had to empty dustbins, check fire hydrants, sweep the roads, everything.

"We were fortunate during that spell because my mother had about four lodgers. All the other men had gone but at that time they were building the tunnel from Burnbanks - well, the end of Haweswater - to Longsleddale and she'd four men staying, they were well-paid and very good with us. They used to take us out."

The 1933 minutes of the Manchester Corporation Water Works Committee record that in 1931 some men at Burnbanks had been given work on 'Contract B' (the Mardale Tunnel and Longsleddale works) but had now been discharged and were unemployed. Since they could not afford their full rent it was reduced by 50% in line with reductions for other unemployed and partly employed tenants.

Meanwhile Mr Jameson was re-appointed as Resident Engineer at a salary of £800 per annum with free accommodation.

John and Joyce Thompson who farm Eastward, close to Burnbanks, were interviewed for the Bampton Millennium Book, *Ploughing in Latin*. John told us then: "In 1936 things were really bad. People were really poor then. They got through it most of them, but there were chaps up on the dam there and they were out of work. They would do anything to make a copper. We had one or two round here. We used to give them a bite of whatever we could. They had families to keep."

Bobby Eastham tells us that the Headmaster at Bampton School, Dougie Thornton, made part of the (school) field into allotments: ".. he put two lads to each one, especially when the dam was closed, it was hard times, he used to let us take vegetables and potatoes, home and sell them."

We know that eventually the situation improved a little and work on the dam began again but in the early 1930s no one knew this. The families must have been bewildered to find themselves exiled from the urban life they had known and deposited in what they must have seen as a hostile wilderness. They had accepted this because of the work and now the men must have feared that they might never work again. Work eventually resumed but there were many economies and life at Burnbanks was never quite the same again. During the recession the Waterworks Committee even apparently thought of reducing the size of the dam to save money. Things settled down but there were always economies because of the very difficult national economic situation. The proposed £10 million scheme was pared down a more modest £1.5 million scheme. The Times reports in March 1934: *The Manchester Corporation Waterworks Committee today decided to complete the truncated scheme for the development of Haweswater. The total estimated cost is £252,000 (in addition to £1,211,000 already spent)...The work will start in two or three months.*

ENLARGING A CITY'S LAKELAND WELL

Picture from The Herald, 1937

Donald Bird above Haweswater dam 1938

The great dam across the head of Haweswater, in the Lake District, which will provide a new reservoir for Manchester, is rapidly taking shape. When completed the dam, 1,550ft. long, will rise to a height of 120ft.

'Lakeland's Great Dam is Rising' News Chronicle August 1938

Haweswater dam nearing completion in 1939

BAPTISMS solemnized in the Parish of Mardale in the County of Westmorland in the Year 1935

	When Baptized.	Child's Christian Name.	Parents Name. Christian.	Surname.	Abode.	Quality, Trade, or Profession.	By whom the Ceremony was performed.
B. 21 Dec 1934	1935 January 6th No. 177.	Dennis Edward Charles	James Lilian	Waters	Burn Banks Bampton	Labourer	Frederick W. Parham Vicar
B Dec: 17/34	January 13th 1935 No. 178.	Maureen	Fred Margaret Ellen	Lowis	Marshall Terrace Shap.	Quarry Worker	Frederick W. Parham Vicar.
1935.	Easter Day April 21st No. 179.	Raymond Cyril	William and Annie Evelyn	Holliday	Burnbanks Bampton.	Labourer.	W. H. Cormack Incumbent of Bampton & Mardale
	Trinity VI July 28 1935. No. 180.	George Ernest	Thomas Richard and Muriel Evelyn	Crabtree.	Burnbanks Bampton	Labourer.	W. H. Cormack

A photocopy of the last page of Mardale Church Register showing the details of the last four Christenings to be held in the Church prior to the Farewell Service on Sunday, 18th August 1935

Church

The Missioner, who had been appointed to serve the community in 1930, left when many of his congregation had left and probably Manchester was unwilling or unable to continue to pay him. He had played an important role in the community. He was replaced by a succession of priests of different denominations led by the Vicar of Bampton who took services in rotation.

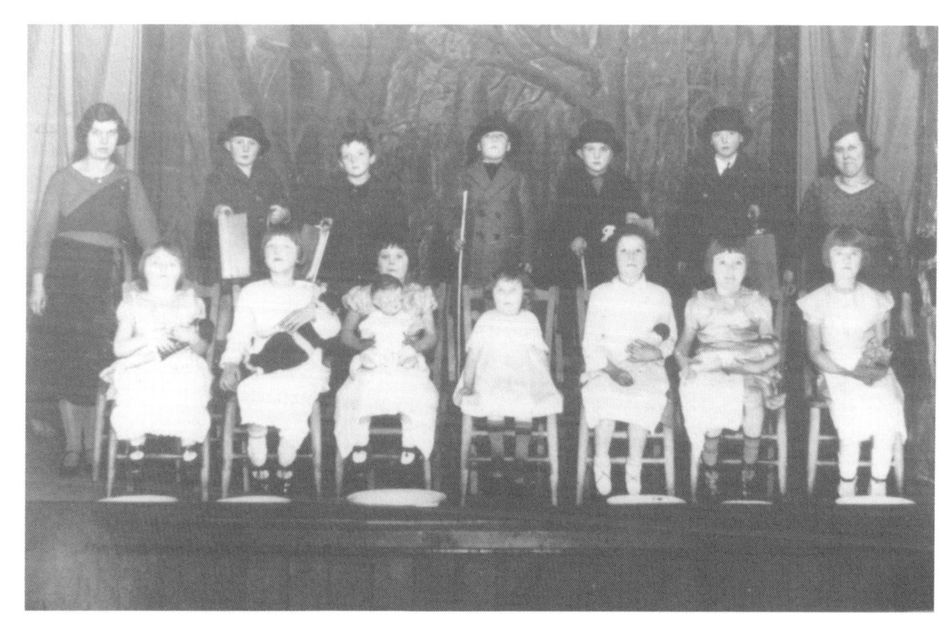

A Sunday School show Christmas 1934 - Louise Eastham, the teacher, with children. Boys: Eric Jewel, Billy Crabtree, Billy Toone, Tommy Moore, Richard? then Ivy Roon. Girls: Margaret Wilson, Betty Thompson, Lily Walters, Aletha Moore, Laurie Wilson, Mairghread MacColl.

Mairghread Sharp tells us: "Some walked to the tiny church at Mardale - three miles. My sister was christened in Mardale Church one of the last before they took it apart. Yes, we went to Sunday School in the Mission Hall. We learned prayers and sang hymns and (there were) talks. There were exciting activities at Easter and Christmas. We had a gigantic Christmas Tree in the Recreation Hall with a gift for every child in our village, organised by the Women's Guild. Mr Jameson paid a lot towards this."

Mrs Olive Hindmarch, her daughter-in-law informs us, used to teach in the Mission Sunday School, up until 1940 and then at Bampton Methodist Chapel. Mrs Nanson remembers attending Sunday school in the mission hall at Burnbanks which she says is now the village hall at Thirlmere. Although her recollections of that are vague she remembers Mrs Hindmarch being involved and probably playing the organ. Bill Rawlings remembers the Mission and some rivalry between Church and Chapel: "Well we called it the chapel, we didn't call it the mission, so it was the Right Reverend Wilfred Cormack, he had to have his right name, the Reverend Willy Cormack. He used to do services there and also somebody from the chapel - they were lay preachers - Dougie Thornton was one, he was a lay preacher.

"I used to go down to (sing in the choir at Bampton) - and of course my grandmother I suppose she got me to go to church, I don't know. I used to go down to morning service and evening service every Sunday. Funerals we would walk in front of the (*coffin*). I can remember two or three times we'd have our surplices and cassocks on and I think there was one particular instance where we walked down when some of the graves from Mardale come down and were buried in Bampton as well as Shap.

"(*Then*) I went to the chapel because of Harry Toone, I think they took me to go there because they were struggling, and then he (*Rev Cormack*) came and got me back again and I finished up down there. Yes, come to see my granny and read the riot act so then I had to go back again."

Louise Eastham with three little girls on a Sunday School outing to Allonby

In his interview, Mr Eastham recalls: "It was Church of England one week as far as I remember, and Methodist the other. And I can remember Mr Dargue from Thornthwaite Hall, and the schoolmaster, Dougie Thornton, and Bailey from Shap, I think he was a butcher, and they used to come and preach. I can remember going at half past six, that's when my mother would be free to go after they'd had their meal at night. It was very good. And my sister, Louise, I think she ran Sunday school for a while as she got older. They had an organ. Yes. Louise used to play a bit."

Walter Twigg was persuaded to join the church choir: "The vicar got Tom and I in the choir.... Ruddick. 'Peg-leg' we used to call him (the vicar), 'cause he had a wooden leg! He said, 'You don't have to sing, because I know you can't sing, neither of you, but just make the numbers up."

Women from the chapel outside 1 and 2 The Oaks L to R: Sheila Dixon, Olive Hindmarch, Grace and Margaret Brunskill (Naddle Farm), Annie and June Holliday

Mrs Sylvia Hindmarch also tells us what she knows about the Mission: "The mission was in the wood just as you come into the village on your left, through the little wicket. I think it would be 1940 when that would close because George's mother was presented with a clock and she was also presented with a bible by the Sunday School and also a little hymn book which we still have, with her name in and who presented it to her. It was the Advisory Committee. She used to go and teach the children in Sunday school and she also used to play the organ in the mission. So it was a little thriving place as well because it was for all religions was the mission, but that was taken down before we came up here and it is now the dance hall at Thirlmere."

The lych gate at St Patricks Church, Bampton Grange, which was a gift from Manchester Corporation for all the inconvenience the project had caused. Left to right: James McCormick, Dan Lamb, John Hutchinson, Rev Day, Ben Martin, Bill Holliday, Sid Wear at the opening of the new gate.

A Burnbanks concert

Shopping and provisions

It was just this great big wooden counter and everything was behind, you just had to ask for everything. Oh the store, it was a well stocked store as well. I can remember as a kid - and I can't remember the peoples' name - but I used to go in the back and play with his son and he'd great big cheeses like that, you know, we used to roll them. They were all in hessian. Ay, they were like blooming wagon wheels they were. And he used to have his piano string, you know, and he used to bring it out there and cut it in chunks.

We also had the Co-op wagon came once a week. The Co-op traveller, salesman, he would come up round the big huts and Granny used to buy a bag of flour, a hundredweight of flour, and stuff like this. You got it in bulk. And she always bought that through the Co-op every week. Went in the larder - quite a big larder. When nothing could get up there for a fortnight we could have still lived.

Bill Rawlings

The original Burnbanks shop had been set up as a non-profit making venture with goods sent from Manchester and sold at cost price. George Hindmarch pointed out: "Manchester paid them say on a Friday night and they'd have all the money back by Monday, with drink, groceries and everything."

But this subsidising of provisions proved too costly and was eventually replaced by a new shop, rented out to a local proprietor who ran it as an ordinary profit-making business.

Mr and Mrs Wilkinson, who ran the store, with their daughter Marjorie and their son Ronnie and his wife and child

June Nanson writes: "I do remember the shop which was located up the back road. It was run by Mr and Mrs Wilkinson and they had a daughter, Marjorie, and a son, Ronald. They became good friends of my family. My brother and I were each given a penny every Saturday morning and hastened to the shop where we spent ages choosing our sweets. It was surprising how much a penny bought - 16 aniseed balls I am told!"

Jean Newhouse who now lives at Milnthorpe wrote to us saying that her father Darwin Leighton, a grocer in Highgate, Kendal, rented the village shop at Burnbanks and supplied groceries for the families in the 1930s. She writes: "The shop was a semi-detached house, in the other house my Dad put in a manager and his wife to look after the shop. But before they arrived I stayed there with my two sisters, Betty and Frances for two weeks in June. Sometimes we used to walk to the village of Mardale at the head of the valley, the road then was on the right hand side of the lake, opposite to the present road. There was a lovely old church, and in the graveyard there was a very old yew tree, which was cut down. My Dad was given some of the wood, he had it made into a pair of candlesticks, unfortunately I do not know what happened to them."

Hughie Davins remembers Burnbanks shops: "There used to be a little hut at the end of the road leading down to the dam workings where the men could buy tobacco & cigarettes and soft drinks, sometimes I would arrange to meet my Uncle there during his lunch break and he would buy me a bottle of pop and crisps while he had a smoke and asked me what I had been doing. There was also the general store on what we called the top road, I used to run errands there for Mrs Eastham if there was anything she wanted, they seemed to sell everything and I always enjoyed going into the shop."

Bill Rawlings also remembers another food supplier: "I think where Mrs Hindmarch lives now I think that's where 'Gobby' Wilson lived. I think it was her that, on a Friday during the recession, she used to make meat and potato pies and people used to go and buy them."

He recalls the other tiny village shop: "And then just across from that (the works) was a little tobacconist and sweet shop and I think a little post office. I think she sold stamps and stuff. But that's where we used to get our chocolates and sweets."

Bobby Eastham remembers all the different delivery vans. Taylors of Penrith brought coal, Harrington's of Penrith delivered meat, as did the Co-op. Southworths came from Shap with a general store and Lesley and Fred Leighton from Shap ran a drapery department on the back road in Burnbanks, near the general store at the top of the hill.

He also tells us that, while he won a scholarship and went to Briggs' Commercial College in Brunswick Road, Penrith, his sister left school at 14 and worked in the shop: "She was the first one to open a shop, which belonged to Douglas's. She actually worked in there before she left school selling papers and cigarettes for all the men going to work."

Sylvia Hindmarch also informs us that H V Douglas had the wooden paper shop up near dam which was open for half an hour in morning and half an hour at night. She tells us: "Louie Eastham opened the shop before going to school and after leaving school - it was the only job she ever had."

And there were other ways of obtaining provisions - Bill Rawlings recalls: "If you went haymaking you never got paid cash, no, just in kind - a bag of potatoes or something like that."

Burnbanks residents with one of the delivery vans

Memories of a delivery van boy

I was actually born at Armathwaite and moved to Rosgill in 1935. The reason I suppose was my father's employment, and I went to school at Rosgill and eventually left and started work at a private firm in Shap here, who were general merchandisers. We supplied cattle foods and you name it we had it, and if we hadn't it we would get it for you, the boss was like that. And, in those days we had a big travelling van, which I was with, not as a driver, but as a boy.

And we went to Burnbanks at that particular time every Saturday morning. And when I first started going there, of course, the place was in its heyday, if that's how you might have put it, and quite a very happy and thriving congregation lived there. There was a mission hall there as well and a village hall, and what they termed as the canteen which was a club, licensed club, and there was a general store, a newsagent's and also the surgery which was attended I think about twice a week. And it was quite a cosmopolitan population there because of the nature of its work. Lot of Irish people that came there, and a fairly quick turnover of population, you know by the very nature of the job.

John Graham, Shap

One of the vans that visited Burnbanks with supplies

Also on the subject of shops, Mrs Sharp remembers that one of the men killed in an accident at the dam had two children, one boy and one girl: "The boy was still at school in Penrith Grammar but the girl was given the management of the little shop at the far end of the village, which sold sweets, cigarettes and newspapers. She was called Rosie and she stayed in her little shop for the next seven years, the mother kept her house – number 8 it was (Mrs. Cuthell). The shop was quite a little gossip centre, all the men bought their newspapers on the way to work, also their Willie Woodbines."

Margaret Higson wrote that she loved visiting Rosie's sweet and paper shop at the dam end of the village on the bottom road and she also recalled Wilkinson's store on the top road. She also mentions the travelling traders: "We were fortunate in the number of travelling shops: Southworth's on Saturday with lovely butter; Colin Cannon with milk plus butter-milk on Saturdays; Mr and Mrs McGuiness from Shap brought fresh vegetables on Fridays; Douglas from Penrith with general groceries and bread and the

Co-op with a previously ordered supply once a month. The meat, during the war used to come from Penrith by bus, George Coulson (or Michael) used to put the packages on the wall as we drove along. The bus used to come from Penrith to Askham via Lowther Park as the road between Eamont to Askham was used for tank practice and was out of bounds. Every now and then a Mr Clay used to come to see if dad wanted measuring for a suit….."

Some homes began to grow their own produce in allotments. Mr Eastham says: "We did have an allotment for a while. Not so far away from the tennis courts. Easter, Good Friday and that was always putting taties in."

Bill Rawling's grandfather kept an allotment: "Now the other side was all allotments going right down to the edge of where the works was, you know like one, two three, four, there must have been about thirty allotments there. Granddad's plot was just beside the bowling green - he was the bottom one. Yes, he used to grow his own onions, his own potatoes and things like that. We had a big deer fence up to stop the deer coming in."

Walter Twigg and his pals played a prank on one allotment gardener: "One thing I can remember, one of my dad's friends, Mr Ted Thompson, he had an allotment and he spent all morning planting cabbage and us three lads - me, my twin brother and Alan Malpass - sat on the bank and watched him. When he went for his tea, we went to the allotment and turned everyone of his cabbages upside down - replanted them upside down. He was not a happy man about that! I think that got us a good little leathering from our fathers."

And there was always food to be harvested from the fields and hedgerows. Margaret Higson remembers picking wild raspberries for jam and mushrooms and nuts.

Tommy Toone and Charlie Squires standing by an allotment

Canteen and recreation hall

The canteen and recreational hall at Burnbanks in 1930

Arthur Cannon came to the village of Burnbanks in 1937 at the age of 14 to live with his 24 year-old brother Colin. Colin had started out as boots boy at the Greyhound Hotel at Shap, where he eventually became the youngest licencee in the country acting as temporary landlord until Bob Daffurn took over after he left the Dun Bull in Mardale, which was demolished to make way for the dam. Colin and his daughter, Margaret, eventually took over The Crown and Mitre at Bampton Grange in about 1967. When Colin applied for the job running the club at Burnbanks he was apparently most surprised when he was called to Manchester for the interview and, not being married, to get the job with free living accommodation. It certainly provided his sisters and young brother with a good home.

Two of Colin's sisters helped with the running of the club while another sister went to London to work as a secretary for the King's physician and later had a very successful career in the RAF. The minutes of the Manchester Corporation Water Works Committee record that *'Managers were appointed for the Wet Canteen at a joint wage of £6 per week'.*

Social life centred on the main entertainment hall, a large wooden building not made by the firm that made the houses. It stood in the part of the village which is now completely gone, next to a similar building which was the works canteen. Bampton was only a mile or so away and the Waterworks Committee was very conscious of the need for Burnbanks to be on good terms with its neighbour so the entertainment hall was run with a view to keeping the workers there in the evenings. It was run like a Working Men's Club and secured a licence to sell alcohol to its members.

Arthur describes the premises: "The club was one large room with a long bar on the public side at the front of which, at ground level, there was sawdust and spittoons which the navvies used. There was also a best room for senior staff. The beer barrels on stillages were in a concrete ground floor beer cellar, kept cool with water sprinklers spraying on them. Beer arrived on a regular basis to Shap station, mainly Tetley's of Leeds, and was delivered by Jack McCormick, Bampton Grange, on the back of his lorry."

Inside the recreation hall

He recalls that the club had about 200-250 members, mainly navvies, who were hard drinkers and could "easily down 12 to 14 pints on a good night". He goes on to tell us: "The premises opened at 5pm when the hooter sounded at work and there would be a mad dash to get in to be first served. Some of the navvies would stay all night until closing time and not go to their lodgings for their evening meal, so much so that Colin had instructions to close the bar at 5.30pm for half an hour. But it made little difference – they just sat on the wall outside until it reopened."

Orphaned at the age of nine, and the youngest of five, Arthur lived first with his Uncle Abraham and family at Stainmore who also, like his father, was a well known farmer. They were staunch Methodists, so living at Burnbanks club among the navvies came as quite a shock.

Mr Cannon reminds us that, since work was hard to come by, people desperate for a job came from far away, such as from West Cumbria. He tells us: "They came with a stick over their shoulder with a red handkerchief and that was all their belongings in there."

He remembers hard-drinking characters such as Marmalade Joe, Nottingham Tom and Major Paddy Burns. He continues: "One evening Marmalade Joe asked for a bottle of Guinness and the men had asked me to fill him a bottle of water. He almost cleared the bottle before he realised that it was water and he then flung the bottle at the mirror behind the bar. My brother Colin was most annoyed and said, 'Arthur, you must never do that again'.

"There were families (as well). I don't know how to describe them really. They were just ordinary-living people .... like the Crabtree family, the Sullivans and the Cooks and they were a close-knit community. Rather strange, if there was any trouble in the club it usually occurred at a break time, at Christmas or Easter and it usually involved a family. My brother was pretty athletic those days and he was soon over the bar and he had a very nice way with him and he used to say, 'Look, I think the best you can do is go home. You've had probably too much'. There was one thing about Colin - he certainly knew how to handle men. He was a very well-respected person."

Arthur recalls one particular bar fight at the club: "I remember there was a big fight one day with this flagman. He was only a little man, Bill Kirby, and the other chap was quite a strong man – he was a big tough man from Carlisle, employed in the blacksmith's shop. But this little man, Kirby, when the other man had had a few drinks he challenged him to a fight. This was outside the club and I've never seen anything like it, never since or before: he just absolutely hammered this man's face, and that, for, oh, it must have been five minutes. Well that plumber man, he went back to his cubicle and he wasn't seen for about a week or a fortnight, recovering from his injuries. There would be no pay for him. No, if you were ill, if a navvy was ill, as I say you only had this little cubicle to live in – there wasn't room for a chest of drawers, just the bed, that's all he had. And there was no such thing as sick leave."

The Cannons were originally a farming family and Colin apparently kept up his interest in farming – cattle in particular: "He used to buy cattle and he would have them rented out with various farmer friends and then at the back end of the year he used to have a sale. He was very knowledgeable. He could sell a cow or a calf and years after he could recognise it in the fields. And the stories I used to hear from him with other farmers when they came to see him. Probably they were thinking of sending the cattle to the auction mart and he would say, 'Well, don't you think, Tommy, if I gave you so much now it would be better that way. You've got the expense of getting it there, then if it isn't sold you've got to bring it back home again. I'll tell you what…' Anyhow, these discussions used to go on well past midnight. My sister, Binnie, used to say, 'Well I'm going to bed'. He liked the country life, he liked farming."

We also learn from Mr Cannon's recollections that there was definitely a class divide at Burnbanks, not only in the housing but also in the club: "I helped out sometimes when I shouldn't have done and that's where I gained a lot of experience of the characters of people, people who had a bit of money. They used to be rattling their money around in their pockets. At the best end you were classed as a – well, it was for the bosses really, the best end of the club. That was a separate room entirely. The separate room was if you were a foreman joiner or decorator, you were in there, you didn't really want to mix with the navvies. Some people that were senior didn't mind but others liked to be aloof, away from the rest."

Bill Rawlings also talks of the canteen: "I can't describe the canteen because I was too young to go in but I used to go in. It was Hazelhurst, he had it, Mr Hazelhurst, and the only thing I can remember - because I was never old enough, of course, well it was pulled down before I was drinkable age, I don't say I wasn't drinking before drinkable age, mind. But I used to go and give him a hand. He had chickens - you pass Naddlegate and you come up and just before you go up a little bit of a hill into Burnbanks, that little field there, he had that as a chicken run on the right hand side. He had his hens and I used to go and give him a hand and he used to get bread and stuff and put it in buckets and feed them, and I can remember going in and seeing all the stills with the barrels on. It was a long building just along there.

"Oh beer, yes, and spirits, oh ay they drank quite a bit of beer. It was a hotch-potch in the weekend. Grandad Toone, how the heck he lived as long as he did I don't know, every night he went into his bedroom about seven or eight o'clock, into bed, and a pipe and he used to be smoking that pipe until he went to sleep. Any night - Monday, Tuesday, Wednesday, Thursday, Friday, or maybe Thursday, and then it was Friday, Saturday, over to the canteen, coming in rolling and then same ritual, didn't go out again for another drink until the weekend again and I think there was a lot like that."

Bobby Eastham remembers that on top of being a carpenter his father had other duties: "But also, on top of that, he was responsible for recreation, he did look after the recreation room where they played billiards and snooker and cards and dominoes. Again, mainly used a lot more in winter than in the summer, because in the summertime he also looked after the tennis courts and the bowling green."

It was important to try to create a real community at the Burnbanks village because most of the people living there had left behind their homes and work here was going to continue for a number of years. There were film shows, Workers Education Association evening classes in subjects such as Shakespeare and industrial history and theatrical performances including pantomimes in which many inhabitants took part. The WEA even sent a teacher from Penrith Grammar School on Tuesday evenings to run a drama class. The letters below were sent from Mr Jameson about these classes in 1938, revealing some social tensions.

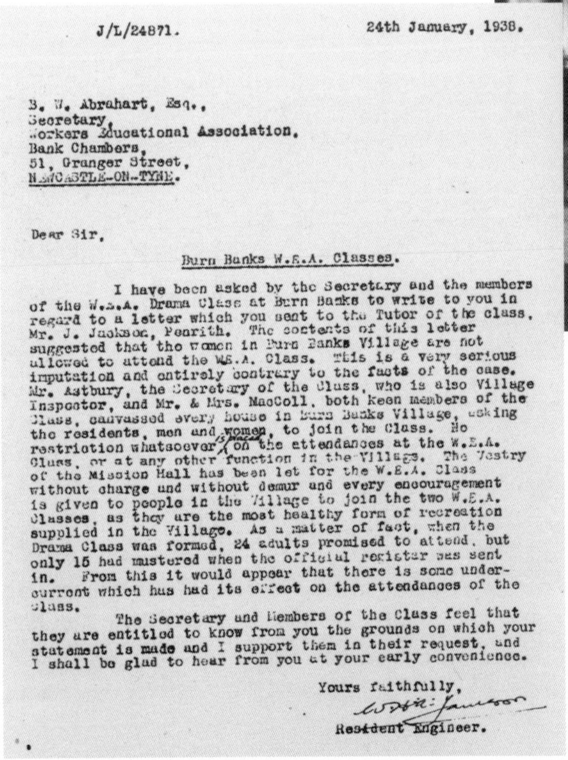

J/L/24871. 24th January, 1938.

B. W. Abrahart, Esq.,
Secretary,
Workers Educational Association,
Bank Chambers,
51, Granger Street,
NEWCASTLE-ON-TYNE.

Dear Sir,

Burn Banks W.E.A. Classes.

I have been asked by the Secretary and the members of the W.E.A. Drama Class at Burn Banks to write to you in regard to a letter which you sent to the Tutor of the class, Mr. J. Jackson, Penrith. The contents of this letter suggested that the women in Burn Banks Village are not allowed to attend the W.E.A. Class. This is a very serious imputation and entirely contrary to the facts of the case. Mr. Astbury, the Secretary of the Class, who is also Village Inspector, and Mr. & Mrs. MacColl, both keen members of the Class, canvassed every house in Burn Banks Village, asking the residents, men and women, to join the Class. No restriction whatsoever is placed on the attendances at the W.E.A. Class, or at any other function in the Village. The Vestry of the Mission Hall has been let for the W.E.A. Class without charge and without demur and every encouragement is given to people in the Village to join the two W.E.A. Classes, as they are the most healthy form of recreation supplied in the Village. As a matter of fact, when the Drama Class was formed, 24 adults promised to attend, but only 15 had mustered when the official register was sent in. From this it would appear that there is some undercurrent which has had its effect on the attendances of the Class.

The Secretary and Members of the Class feel that they are entitled to know from you the grounds on which your statement is made and I support them in their request, and I shall be glad to hear from you at your early convenience.

Yours faithfully,

W. H. Jameson

Resident Engineer.

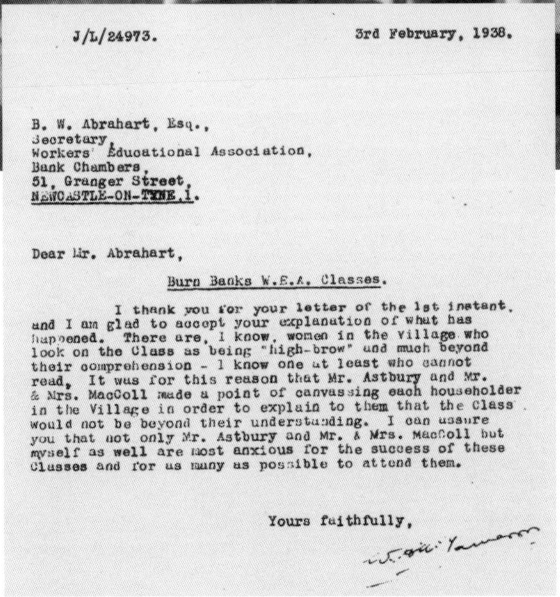

J/L/24973. 3rd February, 1938.

B. W. Abrahart, Esq.,
Secretary,
Workers' Educational Association,
Bank Chambers,
51, Granger Street,
NEWCASTLE-ON-TYNE, 1.

Dear Mr. Abrahart,

Burn Banks W.E.A. Classes.

I thank you for your letter of the 1st instant, and I am glad to accept your explanation of what has happened. There are, I know, women in the village who look on the Class as being "high-brow" and much beyond their comprehension - I know one at least who cannot read. It was for this reason that Mr. Astbury and Mr. & Mrs. MacColl made a point of canvassing each householder in the Village in order to explain to them that the Class would not be beyond their understanding. I can assure you that not only Mr. Astbury and Mr. & Mrs. MacColl but myself as well are most anxious for the success of these Classes and for as many as possible to attend them.

Yours faithfully,

W. H. Jameson

Many Burnbanks women were in Bampton WI. In this picture Mrs Barbara Martin is on the right next to Ada Preston with Marion Bowness and possibly Olive Hindmarch. Jinny Noble (2nd L and Ethel Noble (4th L)

A concert in the early days at Burnbanks with Louise Eastham 3rd from the left on the back row.

There were regular dances attended by young people from Bampton and even further afield. Mairghread Sharp describes Burnbanks social life: "There were sixpenny 'hops' in the recreation hall on Friday nights. The piano was played by Mrs Pugh from number 6 Burnbanks, who also gave piano lessons. The floor was hung on chains and highly polished and a stage at one end with changing rooms and toilets, curtains and footlights. At the other end were billiard tables and all kitchen tea-making amenities. Tuesday and Saturdays a mobile cinema van brought us movies - black and white of course and very noisy with squeaks and crackles and the hissing of the big wheels going round. We saw Boris Karloff horrors and Felix the Cat cartoons. Some people came from surrounding farms especially children. The recreation hall was up the front road opposite the tennis courts. Then there was the wet canteen further up where the men could drink beer, play darts and cards etc. I never was allowed near there."

Bobby Eastham recalls: "Then there was the canteen. The dance hall was one of the best in the area. Well known. We used to get busloads from Penrith coming out for them. There were bands, four-piece bands. There was Kitchen's from Penrith and there was Jackson's from Thirlmere and there was Wishart's from Penrith, There were six-penny hops on a Friday. And fivepence for a pint of beer. There was a class end, one for the workers and then there was one for the super-annuated people."

Jackson's band from Thirlmere. Tom on drums, John (leader) on accordion, Eddie on paino and Isaac Small from Cockermouth on trumpet. John was a relation of Ray Holliday and was still alive in 2004 aged 98

Arthur Cannon also recalls how good Burnbanks dances were "The dances were that good I've seen them being clapped, and the dances not finishing, until 2.30 in the morning and people still went to work the following morning at 7.30! And there were only two cars in the village: Colin had one and Texters had the other. And Colin probably did about four to six journeys to Askham and Lazonby with different car loads. You had a long wait after the dance finished if you were one of the last to be picked up. He had a Standard 12 and they used to get eight in it. How we did it I don't know."

Apparently many couples met at the Burnbanks dances, including George Hindmarch's parents. His widow, Sylvia, who still lives at Burnbanks, explains: "People from Penrith came to the dances, oh yes. Because now you hear of people (celebrating) golden weddings or they're passing away and they met at the dance hall at Burnbanks. I mean it was a really really popular place for people. But the canteen is now the dance hall at Eamont Bridge and the dance hall went to Cliburn and only just last couple of years it was taken down when they got lottery money to build a new one."

Bill Rawlings remembers going to watch silent movies: "Once a week we used to get … silent films. Now whether we got talkies in there later I don't know but I do remember we used to have the silent films and they used to come once a week, to the recreation, yes. It was quite full. Took us about thrupence to go in."

June Nanson also recalls films being shown in the recreation hall: "Well we had a cinema - my mother used to take me to see some of the films there and of course there were dances and then there was the canteen where the adults could go and have a drink."

Margaret Higson also wrote of film shows: "I particularly remember 'The Invisible Man'. We had to take our gas masks to many shows etc. at the Village Hall so that must have been after 1939."

Maighread Sharp remembers her mother doing the catering at social events: ".... we'd entertainment, we'd concerts, pictures and dances, big dances, 8 o'clock till 2 o'clock, which were supper dances, and they used to cover the snooker tables with boards. My mother was responsible for the supper. The big hall was also used for whist drives and other entertainment."

There was apparently a Girls Club in Mission Hall where one of the activities was embroidery. The following is a report of a concert at the recreation hall (date and publication unknown).

HAWESWATER WORKERS ENTERTAINED.

Nearly 200 of the inhabitants of Burnbanks, Haweswater, were present in the recreation hall on Monday evening, when the third of a series of concerts was given by the Kendal Vagabonds. Solos were also sung by Mrs. J. O. Bowe, Otterbank Farm. The concert was arranged by Miss M. Douglas, Kendal. The number present constituted almost half of the population of the village.

The hall has heating accommodation for 300 people and 400 can be accommodated when the floor space is clear. The hall is at the south end of the village, and is used for dancing and concerts. In the billiard room there are two full-sized billiards tables. Another place of interest during the dark nights is the reading room, which contains many books. These are returned to Manchester periodically, and a new stock is sent. Up to the present time the inhabitants have not been fortunate enough to have any cinematographic pictures shown, but the first silent film was to be shown last night, and weekly visits by a travelling cinema are considered very probable.

The total amount taken on Monday was £7 5s., which will be devoted to a fund for Sunday School prizes after expenses have been deducted.

A service was conducted at the Mission on Sunday evening by the Bishop of Carlisle, at which there were nearly 170

Newspaper article, date unknown

School

Twenty Burnbanks children absent. In reply to my telephone call, the Attendance Officer visited us, took the names of the absentees and went to raid Burnbanks.

From Bampton School Log Book, 2nd July 1931

The building of the dam and the model village brought an influx of children into the valley, Bampton School numbers more than doubling within three years. Although at one stage there had been discussions about building a new school at Burnbanks, in the end Manchester Corporation decided to provide a large wooden building at Bampton School to house the influx of children at Burnbanks. This could be divided into three classrooms by sliding panels. The difficulties encountered by school staff in trying to successfully educate a growing and constantly changing population of children were noted in a report of His Majesty's Schools Inspector in 1933: *The headmaster and his assistants have applied themselves conscientiously to their duties and the standards of work ... have been well maintained in spite of serious difficulties. One of the worst of these has been the frequent changes amongst the children. Although the number on the books is now 102, no fewer than 134 new children have been admitted since the influx began. Another difficulty has been the question of discipline; a third the poor attendance of some of the children. Parental indifference appears to have been to some extent responsible for this.*

Bobby Eastham went to Bampton School. He explains: "And the headmaster there at that time was a chap called Dougie Thornton, who was assisted by Maggie Winster from Shap, Ethel Noble, Marjory Longstaff who lived at Knipe, and a chap called Billy Preston, who was eventually killed in the RAF. He (Mr Thornton) was a good master. It was no trouble for me going to school there. He had two sons, one was John and one was Hugh, and Hugh had some illness, some skin disease, and at times he was off school. And when I had finished my lessons, he used to send me in to play with him when I should have been at school."

Mr Eastham also remembers being in school with the children who had moved out of farms in the valley to make way for the dam: "I went to school with the chaps like Ronnie Hindmarch and Colin Bell that used to go to Mardale School, and eventually when they came to Bampton School when everything was closed down, the church and the Dun Bull and everything, I went to school with them."

Mairghread Sharp tells us: "Douglas John Thornton was a great teacher. You hated him at times but he literally beat knowledge into all the children in his care. He never ever hit a girl but his sarcasm was horrible and he really did beat the boys, especially George Veitch and Dennis Sullivan. When I shot up in height to 5ft 8inches when I was 12 or 13 years old I was taller than he was and he humiliated me in front of visitors or inspectors because of it. I would hang my head while he would make reference to 'all brawn, no brain' as I was useless at maths. He did encourage me to read and made me first librarian when he insisted the Education Department let us have a big box of books every month. I read every one of them and kept a loan book until I left there at 13.5 years old."

Mairghread's parents were keen that she didn't mix too much with local children. She remembers games in school: "Very rough games in playground which I did not join in until nine or ten years. There were tops, skipping ropes, marbles and gang warfare. Tough. Girls used to giggle in corners or build houses from sand and pebbles. (My mother)… was very strict and banned me from playing with our village children which made me unpopular."

June Nanson also recalls her Bampton school days: "Well I went to Bampton school of course, starting at five, and we either walked or there was the Hartness's bus, it went at 8 o'clock in the morning, but usually we would walk there which was a good couple of miles there and two miles back. In every sort of weather we ventured out.

"My first teacher at Bampton school was Miss Eva Coward. Then I was taught by Miss Dixon who came with the evacuees from Barrow. She was a very strict but brilliant teacher and I owe the success in my academic life to her tuition. Then I entered Mr Dougie Thornton's class which wasn't a very happy experience. Fortunately at the age of eleven I won a Lowther scholarship and went on to the grammar school in Penrith and was there until I left at the age of eighteen. I travelled on Hartness's bus from Penrith."

Tom Moore recalls having to walk rather than take the bus: "It was a mile and a half from Burnbanks to Bampton School. We walked there every day and walked back. There was a bus but it cost a penny each and there were five of us, and the wages in them days was only between two and three pounds a week which wasn't a lot of money. We took our sandwiches to school, and we put a kettle on the fire to have a cup of cocoa every day."

Haymaking is an important and very busy time in Bampton and the surrounding area. Raymond Holliday remembers the boys at Bampton School being given a card giving them permission to help farmers with the 'haytiming'. He worked one summer at Mr David Dargue's farm at Thornthwaite Hall.

Bill Rawlings has an interesting tale to tell of starting school in Bampton and his years there: "Oh, I remember the first day I went down there (school). I must have been about four years old and Ivy had gone to school and I thought, 'It's about time I was going.' So I went down myself and of course she had to bring me home.

"So I remember going down, starting school. We started as infants in the wooden building. Dougie Thornton, I'll always remember him. And Miss Gornall, she came with the evacuees. No uniforms. Lads would come in clogs. We were pretty well disciplined in those days. I can remember when we first started we'd go down on the bus - there was a bus took us down and we came back on a bus and then as we got older of course I got a bike and I used to bike down to school every day.

"We took our own lunch, always our pack up. There was no kitchen at the time when we started so we took our own lunch. It's patchy is the school because I wasn't all that academic. I can remember one lad that was. Dougie used to tutor him as well, a boy called Ion and I think he ended up in grammar school and went on to higher things, I think. But no, I was just there to do my little bit, do as little as possible and go home.

"He (Mr Thornton) was stretched at times. Oh he was bad tempered. At one particular instance I got a real hammering - he went over the hill actually on that one. We'd gone out at playtime and gone up to where the chapel is, there was a chap had ducks or something there and he had one of these tin baths - he used to keep it with water. Well of course we decided we'd launch it. Well he could see it out of his windows and Cyril Brennand and I were the last to go back in and I got what he called 'Little Jenny', it was one of these things out of the back of a chair and he really lambasted into me and of course as I'm going in, he's hitting, I was bruised from here to there. The old lady (*Grandma*) went down and she made merry hell."

Walter Twigg's brother Tom was apparently deaf, but this was not recognised in school as Walter explains: "Most of the time we were playing truant, my twin brother Tom and me. We'd be stuck in the back of the classroom. School teachers, Douglas Thornton the headmaster, and the other teachers - they wouldn't believe me (that Tom was deaf). I knew. When you're playing about with somebody, you know they're not acting. Mother and Father thought he was just being lazy. So we played truant most of the days. And we'd help the farmer at Littlewater farm - threshing, things like that. And we just loved it. I remember once we asked the postman what time it was, and he told us a bloomin' great lie and we were about an hour in front of ourselves when we got home and she (*mother*) was very cross.

"There'd be gardening two afternoons a week. We had an allotment just beside the football field, so we'd be in there. Tom and I used to get a sixpence for doing the headmaster's weeding after school. That'd put another hour in for us until we got home.

"(*We learned*) nothing. We didn't do percentages. Some of them likely would. But I can never even remember learning percentages or anything like that. it just seemed to be reading, writing and arithmetic - whatever he could get out of us. I can't ever remember doing anything fancy."

Meanwhile, his brother John, was left handed: "That was something else that was wrong. John was the only left-handed one in our family. The headmaster, Dougie Thornton, made him write with right hand, which was totally wrong. It finished up he couldn't write at all!"

Margaret Higson remembers play-time games: "(We used) a large skipping rope for 'pitch, patch, pepper'. And we played ball games against the wall; hand-stands against the wall – skirts tucked in knicker legs; hopscotch over chalked marks on the lower part of the school yard where it was smooth. The sloping part of the yard was loose gravel. I lost skin off my knees and hands regularly and Miss Ball used to let me sit on a chair until they had improved, but it was soon a repeat performance. Tig was another game, and 'the farmer wants a wife' and choosing people by the 'one potato, two potato' method. In the freezing winter water was thrown down in the backyard and used as a slide, making trips to the water lavatories in the far corner of the yard was quite hazardous. There were always conker fights in the autumn..."

When Angus and Margaret Edkins, who arrived at Burnbanks in March 1956, wanted their four-year-old daughter to attend school, they were given the following proviso: "She was quite a clever little lass and she wanted to go but they wouldn't let her because she wasn't five and the old teacher said, 'I can't have them unless they can do up their shoes and fasten their own buttons.' I just looked at her and said, 'She's been able to do that for six months.' So they let her go in the January after she was four didn't they? (The headmaster was) the one who couldn't park a car. He parked his car like a horse, you know, just pointing to the hedge."

George Hindmarch remembered getting a lift to school in an ambulance and that there were five classrooms. During the war, he told us, there were a lot of evacuees and their teachers, Miss Gornall, Miss Pickup and Miss Elliot, came with them.

Audrey Parkin's father, Alec Little, and her husband both worked at Burnbanks, her father as a blacksmith and later her husband as a joiner. Audrey and her husband eventually moved into a Burnbanks house in 1954. She remembers Bampton school: "Well you usually shared a desk. I shared mine with Frank Twigg and I think it was usually boy – girl. I know the classrooms were full."

Audrey, who appears on the front row in the 1948 school photograph, has memories of the strict headmaster: "And I remember one day, Dougie Thornton, for some reason unknown to me, he just whacked his ruler across my hand. He was a nasty piece of work. Mr Aynsley was a nice teacher but he never taught me - he was a quiet chap."

She also remembers walks around Bampton: "And then he, Dougie Thornton, used to take us out for a nature walk; we'd probably go to Chapel Bridge and then you took your drawing paper and your pencil and you'd have to draw it. That was really the highlight of the summer."

Walter Twigg also remembers enjoying school walks: "He used to make us walk round - that was lovely that - walking right round Gatefoot, (*Bampton*) Grange, back in - I loved that. I could walk all day, me, when I was young, but I couldn't run. Now, the school's sports day, they had to run to Knipe Scar. But I've never ever done that."

Packed lunches were the order of the day, apparently, as there was no canteen. But one opened just before Audrey Parkin left Bampton School, aged 11, to go to grammar school. She remembers Mrs Holliday and Ada Preston cooking very good meals in the canteen.

Above: *Dinner ladies at Bampton School| Mrs Holme, Mrs Preston and Mrs Holliday*

Left: *Bampton School 1934*
Back: Herbert Nanson, Norman Ion, Bob Scott, George Veitch, Bill Harrison, Dennis Sullivan, George Campbell, John Thompson, John Thornton. Middle: Vera Kitching, Mary Bell, Emma Mounsey, Sheila Richardson, Betty Thompson, Laura Wilson, Jessie Thompson, Lily Waters, Edna Scott, Ella Noble, Margaret Wilson. Front: Dennis Moore, Raymond Lancaster, Billy Rawlings, Jimmy Waters, Eric Jewel, Tom Erington, Billy Crabtree, Billy Mounsey

Above: *Bampton School 1948 with several Burnbanks children including Back:Eric Richardson, Alan Noble, John Twigg, John Raines, George Hindmarch, Ray Holliday, Kenneth Thompson, Brian Thompson. Middle: Marjorie Scott, Geoff Hindmarch, Elsie Thompson, Margaret Brunskill, Grace Preston, Sheila Dixon, Jinny Thompson, Helen Satterthwaite, Hilda Holme, Janet Satterthwaite, Dorothy Crow. Front: Audrey Little, Gilbert Ion, Colin Hodgson, Brian Twigg, Raymond Crabtree, Ann Longstaff*

Right: *Tasty school dinners*

Boiled Cabbage.

1 wineglass cooking oil.
1 lb. shredded cabbage.
½ onion (chopped up)
1 handful sultanas.
grated nutmeg.
¼ lemon - rind grated.
Salt & pepper

Cook veg and onion very gently for eight mins in the oil & then add other ingreds & cook for further five mins.

A. I. Preston

Bampton School

Time for relaxation at Burnbanks - A stroll by the lake

Fun and games

You feel sorry for the youngsters nowadays who can't run and roam about as we did in the wood and on the fell and by the river. The world was our oyster. We just had a superb childhood.

Mrs June Nanson

From all accounts, the children of Burnbanks had an idyllic childhood. There were seesaws and swings in the village, and like other children in those days, Burnbanks kiddies were expert at making their own fun. They played in the woods, amongst the stacks of logs left to season in the field, made dens, gathered conkers, searched for birds' nests and generally enjoyed a freedom hardly imaginable to today's children.

Mairghread Sharp describes how she learned to swim in Haweswater: "There were two boat houses on the old west side road by the lake. The first one was disused, the wood was rotten but in 1933 I learned to swim there with other children and mothers. My mother tied a clothes rope onto my 6d rubber blow up belt so that I could not get away into deep water and when the rubber ring belt got a puncture and I could have gone under, she panicked and I started to swim without it so my Dad shouted to her, 'Let her swim don't pull her in!' So I did. I was 6 years old.

"All the children (including me) had Woolworths bathing costumes in blue and white or red or white, they cost one shilling. In 1935 they told us we could not swim in the lake water any more because it was for drinking water in Manchester so those who wanted to swim 1936/37/38/39 would walk down, round the edge of Dargue's hay field (Thornthwaite Farm) to reach just below the Frith bridge. Below the waterfalls there was a lovely pool and it was wonderful fun in the hot weather. I was bitten or stung on the bum by a cleg (horsefly) and I could not sit down for three weeks. That was when we were dressing under those overhanging trees."

Margaret Higson also told us that she used to swim or paddle in the river above the Chapel. The girls changing in one field and the boys in another.

Burnbanks children enjoying a paddle in the lake including Kathleen and Cynthia Sandham, Doreen ?, Betty Sandham, Joyce Martin, June Holliday, Mavis Wear

Walter Twigg has idyllic memories of his Burnbanks childhood: "We used to do a lot of walking and ratching about in the little wood right across from the village between there and the new road up to Haweswater. We seemed to spend hours and hours and hours just climbing young trees, young saplings and just losing ourselves for hours at an end."

Tom Moore has happy memories of Sunday walks with his parents: "... depending on the time of year we would pick wild raspberries and brambles, nuts. I remember Dad putting a sheet round the bottom of a nut tree when they were ripe, he would shake the tree and the nuts would drop down, then we would pick them up, put them into a tin and take them home, to have at Christmas. We would also go out mushrooming. There was always plenty to do. It was all very interesting for us."

And he remembers an eel trap: "It was just something we used to play with really. We often used to go down to the waterfall - it (the eel trap) was just above the waterfall at Naddle, and we used to climb on top of it. I can remember the trap door and remember opening it and looking inside. We were always full of mischief."

Mairghread MacColl sitting on the eel trap on the river below the village

Margaret Higson also remembers the eel trap: "We used to cross that field to reach a deeper part of the river and a bridge or go past the Naddle Gate garages to the waterfall – the flat area above is where there was an eel trap."

She also recalls: "There was always a large organised bonfire on November 5th, with a guy and fireworks display on the playing field, finishing with large rip-raps being set off on the way home. And I used to be a member of the Bampton Girl Guides (red-rose patrol) which was run by Mrs Cormack, the wife of the Bampton Grange Vicar. We used to walk over to Ullswater, up Knipe Scar and held May Day celebrations in the vicarage garden with a May Queen (Betty Thompson was the first one and I was the second one in 1943), Maypole dancing, refreshments and games.

"Dad had a lovely voice and used to sing solos in the church, chapel and at village concerts. There were excellent concerts in the village hall. The Christmas parties at school were special as were those at the church and chapel which most people attended. For the younger children, Dr Prentice's son performed magic tricks at the Christmas party.

"Living opposite one of Mr Dargue's hayfields we used to go and help at hay-time. I don't suppose we were very useful but we tried our best and it was good fun. The summer days always seemed sunny and warm, plenty of time for a group of us to go picnics, taking (everything) in a large pram.

"I used to go fishing with George and Dad. And there was a football team which played on the field at the top of Naddle Gate, opposite the triangle. On the narrower side of the stream, Mr. Crabtree kept his hens which Billy let out on his way to school. My brother and myself used to play in that stream (it looks narrower now) and crawl along it under the road to come out in another of Dargue's fields."

Bill Rawlings also has fond childhood memories: "As kids there was always plenty of snow in the winter so we sledged, skated and snow balled. In the spring and summer we played hopscotch, football, cricket and looked for birds' nests. In the autumn we picked hazelnuts and knocked chestnuts down from the trees for conker fighting."

Mairghread Sharp remembers enjoying playing with Angus Duncan and his elder brother, Willie: "Willie used to dig up the mud in the bank at the back of the houses and build his design of a dam, pour the water in the top half and then open the gates of mud and let it run down into the large dam at the bottom."

Local boys often went hunting for rabbits or fishing in the tarns and becks. Bobby Eastham remembers catching tadpoles in a jam jar, fishing and tickling for trout. Bill Rawlings tells us that he enjoyed fishing from an early age: "Well nearly as soon as I could walk, I was a loner and I got a fishing rod and I fished Cawdale, Heltondale, Riggindale, Fordingdale, Mardale, Blea Water, Small Water. (*I'd catch*) one or two - used to get a few perch in Littlewater. I'd just get a few sandwiches and a bottle of cold tea and that would be me off. When it was school holidays of course because I never missed a day off school, never. Harry, he used to like fishing, Harry Toone. He did quite a bit of fishing."

Walter Twigg was also keen on fishing as a lad and remembers catching good perch, especially after he moved up to Drybarrows. Tom Moore recalls fishing in the lake: "And we had to get a licence to fish the lake. We had to write to Oakham in Rutland. One of the Lowthers lived there at the time."

Many older locals wistfully recall that the becks were then full of fish. Mr Rawlings mourns their demise as the legacy of extracting so much water: "United Utilities, they've ruined it. I can walk on spots and you can see where they've diverted (*water*). They're pinching every little bit of water out the hillside, they're shoving it in little rivulets that used to be there but have gone because they're draining it away. It breaks my heart to see Cawdale and Heltondale as low as they are. There's no fish there now."

Walter Twigg was also very keen on fox-hunting, and the famous Mardale Hunt was right on the doorstep: "Yes, I would say a couple of times I can remember very vividly - when we'd loose the hounds up out of the Bullwagon at Naddlegate, I'd be with Joe Wear, the huntsmen, right from there right till he'd finish up at Bampton Jerry at night and then I'd walk back to Drybarrows. But I could keep up with Joe Wear all day long."

Margaret Higson remembers the hunt: "I remember the hunt coming – men in redcoats going up the crags at the side of Haweswater with their hounds, being followed by people on foot. The hounds were kennelled in the buildings opposite Mr Noble's farm."

Mardale Shepherds Meet November 1935 including l to r: Betty Bell, Tom Robinson, Tom Bell, Jim Brennand, William Moore, Dan Lamb, Harry Morgan, Lant Noble. Rea Kitchen, Aida Preston, Maurice Bell, Bob Daffurn, Ernie Thompson, Stan Hodgson, Mr Brennand, Joe Weir. Bill Atkinson, Tom Edmondson, Colin Bell, Jack Hodgson, George Bland, J. Wilkinson, Viscountess Lowther. Freddy Kitchen, John Edmondson, T. B. Nelson, Walter Parkin, Dr Jim Thompson

There were also scouts and cubs and Bobby Eastham recalls being a 'sixer' in cubs and that John Texter went with him but John was later killed while serving in the RAF.

Mr Glasson, the Missioner, is on the left (and possibly his son on the right)

Raymond Holliday remembers trips into Shap and Penrith: "We used to go to the pictures but it was either Penrith or Shap (*it would be*) push bike mostly to Shap pictures, on the bus by Hartness's bus to Penrith pictures."

Mrs Nanson also remembers happy childhood games: "I remember playing hopscotch and I remember we used to juggle with two and three balls - we were pretty good at that, and we skipped. And then of course we had games in school which was rounders for the girls and football for the boys.

"....usually after school we trailed home, it took us quite a long time. We went by various routes and then, mainly in the village, we ran wild in the woods and down by the river and had a really carefree childhood."

Hughie Davins also has happy memories of summer holidays in Burnbanks: "As you can imagine coming from the city and never having had a holiday away from Manchester, coming up to Haweswater for a month was like being transported to paradise.

"My uncle of course had to go to work during the day but I soon made friends with the other children and the day was usually spent playing down by the beck or roaming over the fells at the back of the village.

"One of the places where we often used to play was called Colby, it had been an old farm or smallholding on the track above the lake leading towards Measand falls, the buildings had all been demolished of course but we used to build our own dam on the stream alongside.

"The lad I played with most was Donald Bird who was the same age as myself, I got to know him because it was his elder sister who worked for the Easthams. Some of the other children were Billy Crabtree, who had several brothers and sisters whose names I cannot remember, and two brothers whose surname was Wynne. I think the Christian name of one was Dougie.

"At weekends my uncle would take me out and show me various places he thought would interest me and one day he took me over to Pooley Bridge and we went for a sail on the *Raven* which was wonderful, but usually we rambled over the fells or along the lake where he would point out the various birds and other wild life which were very interesting to me."

Hughie Davins with his uncle Stephen Rhodes

Donald Bird and Hughie Davins at Thornthwaite Force, near Burnbanks village

Burnbanks also had a very good football team which played on a pitch just outside the village near Thornthwaite Hall. The hard manual work and good food provided for the work force had made the players very fit so that they were too good for most local village teams.

There was also a bowling green and allotments near the dam. In the summer there were less formal sports days with events suitable for all the family.

Bobby Eastham remembers playing cricket and football but he apparently didn't play football for the actual team. He tells us: "We played every night during football season. When it was light nights, we kicked a ball about for hours and hours, it just went on for two or three hours. Say if there were 14 of you to start with, and you was seven a side, and then there's one come, one went on that side and the next one went on the other side, so you finished up 12-12. Down at the bottom, right opposite the village was a field, next to the bowling green, and we used to kick about in there, and we played cricket on there as well.

"And my father helped - they'd a football team, and he was the secretary for a time. That kept me interested, I was always keen. I always used to go away with them. The football team had a full strip, because my mother used to wash them on top of all the other washing she did. Shap, Keswick, Ullswater, Ambleside, Pennine Rangers, Lazonby - we played all the local teams. They weren't such a good side when my dad was (first) secretary, but after he'd started, about 1937, '38, '39, we won the cup, the senior cup. We beat Shap in the final. We drew 2-2 at Kendal, at Netherfield Park Side, but we beat them at Appleby 2-0 in the replay."

Mr Holliday remembers sometimes playing football for Shap: "I used to push bike up to Shap to play - that was quite a pull up!"

Bowling green at Burnbanks

Haweswater United AFC, Westmorland Senior Cup Winners, 23rd April 1938. Back row: Dick Wilson (committee), George Thompson, Patrick Murdoch, Bill Johnson, Jim Fountain, John Farrell, Bob Shields (trainer), Tim Scott (committee) Front: Jim Cook (first aid), Joe Ridout, Jim Lewis, Harvey Wightman (captain), Alfie Bell, Jake Watson, Harry Toone

Alfie Bell being held aloft, Harvey Whiteman holding cup, Bob Eastham next left to Alfie with hat and scarf on

Bill Rawlings tells us: "And the football pitch…. was at Naddlegate, the field just as you're coming into Naddlegate on the right hand side and that was where we played. When the village was first built the football pitch was in the field across the bottom road with the children's play area, swings and see saw. When the timber started coming down from Mardale the football pitch was moved to Naddlegate.

"That year we (*Haweswater United*) won the Westmorland Cup (1938) I was a mascot, I was dressed up in red and white. There's a little bit about me in there *[shows magazine]*. Oh, although my name is Rawlings when my mother moved down there…. I was left with my grandma Toone, so my name after that was Billy Toone, or Macky Toone as I got nicknamed because Bill was Mac so I did most of my life up there being called Macky Toone. So anybody that does know anything about them all they'll know me. Well we won the Westmorland Cup, yes. I can remember vividly the Lord Mayor of Manchester coming and presenting the medals in the recreation room and I got half a crown. Unfortunately I don't know where the half crown is now. Shook hands with me and gave me half a crown, Alderman somebody, can't remember his name."

Bill also remembers that John Farell who played for Haweswater United came originally from West Cumberland, to work on the dam. He met and married Mr Rawling's aunt, Ivy Toone, and went on to have two sons, Eddie and Laurie.

Football, it seems, was not just for boys! Louise Eastham is in the middle at the back

Bobby Eastham also played tennis: "We'd two tennis courts. I played tennis - all one year I played with a lad called Billy Thompson. We played with Mrs Jewell and Ada Preston, who used to live in the mill at Bampton. Every Saturday we used to have a foursome. The vicar at Bampton then was a chap called Cormack and he used to play tennis and there was a tennis court at Bampton Grange, when you leave the Mitre and go towards Shap and down a little hill - not very far - and then where McCormicks had a garage there and a petrol place - the tennis court was just behind there."

Bill Rawlings recalls: "The bowling green was built up out of the soil (*from the excavation works*). It was a lovely bowling green with a bowling hut and trees. Bear in mind when I'm talking about this I'm only a kid so I never played bowls on it, and it was a flat green, same as Penrith. And then down below that there was the tennis courts, that was to the side going towards the estate office. And then next to that was all this timber they'd put and then the estate office. Oh and the quoits. Now I think that was made from the blue clay that came out of the dam and it was a big clay patch and a stake in the middle, a big iron stake, and you used to have a thing like a horseshoe, if you like, and you used to throw it and the one that got nearest to it won. But if some was too near you'd just try and knock it away. And they would play for pennies and ha'pennies. Also there was a pitch and toss…"

Darts was the favoured sport for young Arthur Cannon, who had a distinct advantage living at the club: "Darts was very popular in the club. I became quite a professional at darts because I played really all weekend. I was playing fictitious names – I was playing against Bill Farrell in my mind, Johnson in my mind. We played with wooden darts with lead in the centre of the wooden dart and they had goose feathers – they were all one, the flight wasn't separate, the shaft and the flight were all made one with a lead barrel or ring depending on the weight of the dart you required. With throwing so many darts at a young age I got very, very quick - so quick that as soon as the first dart had gone in the last dart was following it – you hadn't seen the second dart go in. By that I used to baffle a lot of people. ….and there wasn't very many people that would beat me."

Haweswater United with Lady Lonsdale presenting the cup

Right: *Louisa Eastham and a friend at a Gretna Wedding*

Below: *Out for a walk*

A group of Burnbanks residents relaxing

Transport

Harry Holme and his bus which ran from Burnbanks to Penrith. The young boy is thought to be Leonard, his son

Since very few people had cars in those days, country-dwellers were well-used to walking the few miles to and from Bampton and there was a much better bus service than we have in the valley these days since everyone depended upon it. Mrs Sharp writes: "The Bus came from Penrith three times a day 8am, 10am, 2pm and on Saturdays 5pm and 10pm. The bus would wait 10 minutes before going back to Penrith. School children, at least 20 of them, went to school at Bampton on the 8am bus."

Walter Twigg remembers Ernie Hartness' bus and how uncomfortable the wooden slatted seats were: "Oh! They were hard to sit in. They were terrible to sit on, time you got to Penrith…"

BAMPTON BUS "COMMANDEERED."

Burnbanks Labourers Cause Over-crowding.

A sequel to the alleged commandeering of a bus returning from a Saturday night dance in Penrith by workmen employed on the Manchester waterworks scheme at Haweswater was the charge at Penrith Police Court on Tuesday against John William Blackstock, motor driver, c/o Mr. Holmes, Bampton, Penrith, of conveying a greater number of passengers in a motor bus than the vehicle was licensed or constructed to carry at Corney Place, Penrith, at 11-45 p.m. on 1st November.

Blackstock pleaded guilty and was represented by Mr. C. Arnison.

Sergt. Kennedy said the passengers in defendant's bus were very noisy and were shouting and singing. He stopped the bus and found in it 27 passengers. The seating capacity was 18 and the bus was licensed to carry 20. Defendant said he could not help it as the passengers rushed on the bus.

Answering Mr. Arnison, witness said he was aware that most of the passengers in the bus were Burn Banks labourers and that they were returning from a dance in the Drill Hall.

Mr. Arnison said the defendant had brought a party in to the dance and workmen from Burnbanks took possession of his bus. Some of them were actually in the bus before his own passengers were in. He tried to prevent them from getting into the bus but in spite of his efforts to keep them out, they insisted on getting in and he had no alternative but to proceed with them in the bus.

The Bench ordered the defendant to pay the costs, recording no conviction.

A report from The Herald about an incident on the Burnbanks bus in November 1930

Arthur Cannon remembers: "Last bus was at 10.30pm Saturday which my sister and myself often missed because we were enjoying ourselves dancing at St Andrew's parish hall until five minutes to twelve midnight, and then had to walk the long 10 to 11 miles back to Burnbanks. Happy days!"

Sylvia Hindmarch's late husband George told us how bicycles were the most popular transport for the workers: "Of a night (*after work finished*) bikes that were going down (*along the road*) here were colossal!"

Harry Holme brings an MCWW official, possibly Mr Holme Lewis, engineer and agent, to Bampton

Bobby Eastham recalls getting his first bicycle when he was about ten years of age. It was a Hercules and cost £4, bought from Milburn's of Middlegate, Penrith. Raymond Holliday's mother worked in the canteen at Bampton School for 24 years. He and his sister tell us that she cycled each day to and from Bampton regardless of the weather.

Bill Rawlings worked in the garage at Burnbanks and he tells us: "Going on the top road past the substation there was another four semis, drop down the hill, the Corporation garages, the wooden garages (were there). I used to work in those garages - that's where we had our wagon. But one year there was a man drowned in Haweswater and he was in that garage. They brought him and left in there all one night.

"And they had two big Morris Isis cars. Oh, big cars they were that they used to go down to Penrith and pick the wages up every Friday. They used to be armed, whoever went down. They also picked people up coming from Manchester to Penrith railway station - officials."

Arthur Cannon also told us how, after he moved to Bampton Grange, he would cycle to and from work and that his cat would meet him at the chapel and ride home with him on his shoulders!

Bobby Eastham remembers that, in those days, people would just go on day trips rather than proper holidays: "Well if ever my mother went on a holiday or out at all, it would be a day trip to the Lakes. I can remember my dad organising one to Windermere and it was the Sunday before Sir Henry Seagrave went down on a boat on the lake when he was trying to break the world record.

"Blackpool illuminations and Morecambe illuminations were places that they visited. I can remember Harry Holme running a flat lorry through the week carrying materials and then he'd put a body on it and convert it to a charabanc at weekends. You could only get in on one side and everybody had to file down, move along the seat, it was like a proper charabanc."

Harry Holme with his bus outside the St Patrick's Well, also known then and now as The Jerry

Raymond Holliday recalls trips to Morecambe with his grandfather as a boy. Then later he organised some of the Burnbanks outings: "In the '50s in my spare time I organised trips to Morecambe for the Miss Lunesdale final and to Blackpool for the lights. We hired Hartness's buses from Penrith."

Bill Rawlings tells us: "We went to Morecambe a couple of times, but I think we also went once to Whitley Bay. And it was a big Leyland Tiger I think the bus was, oh it was great that. I don't know whether it was a school trip or a village trip."

Harry Holme's son, Chris, still lives in Bampton. He tells us: "Dad, being Harry Holme, would run a bus service from Haweswater to Penrith, and I think it would probably go on a Tuesday and a Saturday. Anybody that wanted to go to any dances on a Saturday night, Dad would go up there and put on his bus. I can remember one old lady once telling me, 'We used to go all over the spot with your Dad to dances, but the first time he got his bus, a brand new bus, we had to get out at the bottom of the Crears and push it up the Crears.' So the engines weren't quite as powerful as what they are today."

Tony Bell on a Triumph motorbike with Louisa Eastham

Children outside a Naddlegate house

Burnbanks children

Weather

The weather in these remote valleys in the northern Lake District can be harsh, with regular flooding in heavy rain and very often, particularly in years gone by, extremely bitter freezing conditions and thick snow.

In February 1933, it was cold with snow but my father took my mother and me to walk up past village right up on to the old packhorse road and we walked to see the foundations of the new reservoir. Dennis Sullivan and the Thompson boys (were) all sliding on the frozen pool below the tennis courts and it looked like a beautiful Christmas card.

Mairghread Sharp

Bobby Eastham remembers bad winters: "Phew! Ay I walked to Askham for bread. Yes, that would be 1940, would it? I remember Joe walking to Askham. Oh yes, we cut snow out on the concrete road to keep that road open. Everybody went on snow cutting then."

It is possibly this winter or that of 1946/7 that Sylvia Hindmarch's late husband George told us about when we interviewed him at the time of the Millennium: "We'd a man called Billy Douglas used to come with a van. He was ringing the telephone at Bampton Grange and Gilbert Ion answered it. He told him that he'd be at Askham (with supplies) at a certain time. So Mother and them walked to Askham and David Dargue from Thornthwaite Hall took a horse and cart to Askham."

And Bill Rawlings tells us: "In the really bad winter, '40-'41, nothing come through for a week. They started digging out from Burnbanks and they started digging out from Penrith and I think it took them about four days. And we were going to school and I can remember just past - there was a barn, hoggast, it's gone now, you couldn't see above the snow where they'd dug out, it was that deep - it must have been twelve foot high right through where it had drifted.

Snow on the ground at Burnbanks

"Also in those early days we used to get a heck of a lot of flooding as well. I think it's still there - there was a little low wall going to the school where when it flooded we'd to get up on that and we'd to walk along the wall from Bampton Grange to Bampton.

"Oh it (*Haweswater*) was completely frozen over - we were all skating on it. That was about '34-'35. It was a big freeze up. It was thick, yes you could have taken a horse on, it was that thick.

"But also I can remember as the dam was being built there was a nice grassy path right up onto the fell-side from the village and we could walk along - because they'd fenced it all off then because of the blondins and everything - and Lord Lonsdale's boathouse, oh and it was a beautiful place, a lovely green and a jetty round where he had his boat in, it was a lovely place that. And I can always remember standing there and seeing a big perch sailing past and ooh - I think we'd had a really heavy snow fall and it didn't gradually (rise), it flew up, right over the spillway. You get more water from snow when it's thawing out."

George Hindmarch told us that one day when he was just a little boy walking home from school, he was caught in a bad blizzard: "I was a boy for the lassies and I had two lassies – one at each side. Doreen Wilson was one lass – they'd be lassies maybe two or three years older. I weren't so old. Honestly it was terrible. And I managed not to break down (*crying*) until Mother come down to meet me."

Walter Twigg particularly remembers helping the farmer look for sheep in the snow drifts: "I know in the snow, it took months and months and months to dig it out one winter, from Burnbanks to Penrith. we could never see the walls, walk right over the top of them. It was magic. Up at Drybarrows in 1947 we never got to school for quite a long while. And I remember the farmer giving us a big long stick. Stand on top the drift, poke, and poke down to see where we could dig sheep out. Some of them was alive, but very, very few of them, very, very few. You know you could feel them when you were pressing - that there was a sheep under. That was sad because there was thousands died. But we never got to school for weeks and weeks which was great!"

If the school had to close after a really bad snow-fall, Burnbanks children had great fun. Tom Moore, for instance recalls: "All we did was go out into the snow and make tunnels inside and snow houses - that was great fun. I can remember getting up in a morning, and drawing the bedroom curtains and the deer would be looking in at your window. They were only looking for something to eat. Ah, they were happy days. I really enjoyed them."

Delwyn Davies recalls how wet the weather could get in the valley: "My resident chief's home in Bampton was so dilapidated that visitors were given large umbrellas when they went to bed – in case it rained!!"

Margaret Higson recalls: "The trips over Shap Fell in snow and fog were quite tricky, chains on the wheels of our Ford 8 – (*registration number*) AMB 806."

But she also reminds us that the weather wasn't always so bad: "The summer days always seemed sunny and warm. Heat haze used to shimmer over the field in front. The winters seemed long, cold and snowy – walking to and from school quite uncomfortable. Eventually an old ambulance took us to school in the bad winters – I don't remember it bringing us home."

Gerry Dawson enjoys a sunny day at Burnbanks

War

By the time the dam was complete in 1942 the Second World War was in progress and most of the workers had left to join the armed forces or to do other war work.

In 1939 the Manchester Corporation minute book records that the dam and chambers were prepared as air raid shelters for Burnbanks residents.

MANCHESTER CORPORATION WATERWORKS.
HAWESWATER SCHEME.

L. HOLME LEWIS, M.INST.C.E., M.I.MECH.E.
ENGINEER.
WATERWORKS OFFICES,
TOWN HALL, MANCHESTER, 2.

TEL. NO. CENTRAL 3377 (EXTENSION 235).
TELEGRAMS—"WATER, MANCHESTER."

J/M/31096.

'PHONE, BAMPTON 22.

W. H. M. JAMESON A.M.INST.C.E.
ENGINEER—SECTION A.
MANCHESTER CORPORATION WATERWORKS,
BAMPTON,
BY PENRITH.

29th March, 194[illegible]

CITY OF MANCHESTER

TO WHOM IT MAY CONCERN.

The Bearer, MR. VICTOR SLESSOR, has been in the service of the Corporation from 10th March, 1936 to the present date, when he leaves the service owing to being called up for the Army.

He has been employed in general work connected with the construction of the Dam, excavation, etc. and has latterly been employed in and about the Cement Shed and Concrete Mixer.

He has proved himself to be steady and a good timekeeper.

W.H.M. Jameson
Resident Engineer.

Mr Jameson provides a reference for Victor Slessor on his leaving Burnbanks to serve in the army

We'd a radio in the school then and he (Mr Thornton) had us sitting there all in the big hall, all sombre, and Chamberlain was speaking: "I have to tell you..." And that was it - that was the war.

Bill Rawlings

At the age of 17 Arthur Cannon found himself in charge of maintenance as the others were sent elsewhere or off to war. He tells that he was, however, able to call in a Carlisle electrician, Tommy Watson, if there were jobs he couldn't manage alone. He eventually tried to join up himself: "I remember when in 1941 I volunteered for the RAF, and after spending three days at RAF Padgate being called back to work and being severely reprimanded as I was in a reserved occupation – the only person then left on site with any electrical knowledge. Shortly afterwards I repaired on my own the main LV underground cable that ran from the dam to the village substation after it had been damaged by workmen during excavation."

So Arthur stayed at Burnbanks until he was called up in 1942 while others went off to war. He tells us, though, that he was active in the Observer Corps and the Home Guard: "I was a member of both. The Royal Observer Corps was situated in a wooden hut between Burnbanks and Bampton on the left hand side as you leave Burnbanks. I also was a member of the Home Guard. (*One night*) there were three of us and the corporal. He was an ex-World War One serviceman. He would show us how to load and unload a 303 rifle. This is midnight to one o'clock in the morning. The place we're in is the village substation where I used to charge the batteries. It was a concrete/stone-built building. He puts the rounds of ammunition in the 303 and he was giving us a demonstration, ejecting the live bullets and he said to us, 'Whatever you do, always point the rifle away from you, before you hand it back and press the trigger, just in case there is a round left in'. And he did and there was a round left in. We were all covered in dust, we were absolutely shattered. It was fortunate he'd pointed the rifle away from where all the electrical cables were in the substation but we never found the spent cartridge. The thing I remember most is all of us looking at each other and we were covered in white dust – quite an explosion!"

By the time Walter Twigg moved up to Drybarrows in about 1942, he says that people were rapidly moving away. And Raymond Holliday remembers his father going off to war: "First he was in the Home Guard and then he was called up in 1941 and he was in the Second World War till the end of the war."

Young Walter Twigg was highly embarrassed by the gas masks his father provided for them: "Tom and I had them bloomin' mickey mouse ones and I used to hate everybody laughing their heads off at us. It was terrible! I could've screamed! Blimey. Everybody else had a proper one. Where the heck we got them from, I don't know. We had to wear them anyway (even to school – everywhere). He must have got them in a jumble sale, cheap somewhere, my father. They were terrible. My mother, up till a few years ago, she used to still laugh about that."

Tom Moore remembers how families managed when in wartime things were scarce: "They didn't really waste anything in them days, you know, we never took any harm during the war. Our butcher McCormick lived in Bampton Grange. They killed all their own cattle and sheep and that, and so we never really went short, we always had plenty. You could go to the farms, every farm killed a pig, they had plenty of ham and bacon, they made their own butter, there were eggs, so you know, and we never went short.

"My mother made most of our clothes. She did a lot of knitting and sewing, and it was not unusual to see us going to school with patches on your britches and that, and she darned your socks. They do nothing like that today. Everybody was the same, it was during the war time, the stuff wasn't in the shops to buy. People had to make and mend. And in summer, I can remember my mother buying three or four dozen eggs when they were cheap, and putting them into an earthen jar with isinglass and water and that used to keep them fresh until she used them mainly for baking."

He also gives this amusing example of wartime make-and-mend: "A lady was baking Christmas cakes one day, and they hadn't just turned out as she would like and they had sunk in the middle a bit. So she said to my mother, 'Would you like them, could you do anything with them?' So my mother said, 'Yes I'll take them, possibly do some thing with them.' After Christmas the lady said to my mother, 'What did you do with those cakes I gave you?' 'Oh,' she said, 'I steamed them and we had them as Christmas puddings with plum sauce on.' It would be during the war some time, you know, when things were short."

The relatively safe and carefree life in Burnbanks contrasted sharply with the severe bombing and deprivations of living in the industrialised conurbations around Manchester and Liverpool. Betty Jewell was from Bolton but her late husband, Eric talked to her about his childhood at Burnbanks where he lived from the age of two: "It was a very happy young life for Eric. I mean I was in Bolton in the war and there was bombing in Manchester, but Eric used to talk about the lovely times they had up here and they used to chop wood from the trees and go up the mountainside and wander for ages out on the moors and nobody bothered and there was no fear of bombing."

Joyce Aran remembers wartime at Burnbanks: "I remember the incendiary bombs that they dropped and everybody said, 'Oh, they're trying to hit the dam', but they hadn't got the bouncing bomb had they, to hit it with. And we all sat quite happily in these little houses - I mean, if anything had hit it we'd soon have been washed down the valley, wouldn't we? They dropped a lot of incendiaries which absolutely lit up the whole of the fells round the lake, then they dropped I don't know how many - maybe half a dozen bombs. Of course we loved going to get the shrapnel out of the craters when they dropped them. But they never really got anywhere near the dam - I mean, the dam from the air must have looked (*tiny*) and it was never hit. They landed on the fells particularly where the hotel is now.

"I know as well, we never had any shortage of food because my dad working round these farms, every time they killed a pig or a cow or anything he used to come home with the butter and the milk and some meat and whatever they'd made out of the pigs - some sausage and black pudding so we never (*went short*). We had our own hens down the back garden. We certainly didn't go short of food during the war, not like a lot."

Margaret Higson wrote: "During the war, I used to go around with a collecting tin for the 'Free French'. I don't know how I became involved but I can remember my walks with it to Mrs Brunskill at Naddle Farm. We also knitted mittens etc. for the forces."

Tom Moore's father was called up in 1939: "So my mother brought us up during the war. She had five of us to look after. All the women did a marvellous job really at looking after their families."

During these hard times fish and rabbit were important food. Tom tells us: "Yes, (*we caught fish*) mainly perch, but I didn't like skinning them, they were very prickly, but they were nice sweet fish to eat. During the war it was great to have fish. We used to catch rabbits - rabbits were beautiful, I really enjoyed them, you could eat rabbit pie hot or cold."

George Hindmarch remembered collecting tins of corned beef and stewing beef from the Crown and Mitre pub in Bampton Grange during times of war-time rationing. And he recalled that Dougie Thornton kept school allotments, not only across from the school in the present playing field, but also at Bampton Grange, near where the Grange Field houses are now.

Bobby Eastham recalls being left behind while others went off to war: "I can remember Billy Thompson and Thomas Morgan and Billy Jackson, all those people joined up before I did - I felt awful because I was left at home. But the authorities just said, 'Well you're doing a good job taking these houses down', I suppose, and that was it. But then I did go about June 1942. I was twenty one."

Mr Eastham also remembers that when he was stationed in Norfolk he went to meet a Burnbanks friend: "I went to meet John Texter - he was either an air gunner or a wireless operator I think. I was in the RAF in Norfolk, he wasn't so far away and I went to meet him at a place called Thetford one night. We arranged to meet and I waited and waited, and he never came to see me. He'd been shot down, and killed."

In fact John Ashburner Texter died aged 22 in Novemeber 1942 and is buried at Chalandry in France. George and his brother J Henry Thompson were also both casualties of the war, George dying of TB and his brother died while captured by the Japanese and imprisoned in Indonesia.

John Texter on leave from the RAF

Mrs Sharp remembers that some of the women who ran the boarding houses lost loved-ones in the war: "The landladies I know were Mrs Bardsley, Mrs Jewell, Mrs Eastham, Mrs Wilson, Mrs Thompson, Mrs Sullivan, Mrs Riddout and Mrs Toone. Mrs Thompson lost two sons in the Navy; Mrs Eastham lost one son in Air Force; Mrs Sullivan had one son in the Air Force. I don't know if he survived."

And Bill Rawlings remembers that, while working planting trees up the valley during the war, Wellington bombers would fly right down the lake nearly touching the water before lifting up just before the dam face. It could be that these were training flights for the famous Dam Busters.

Arthur Cannon remembers these flights, too as well as some bombing: "I remember once …. they must have been carrying out practice dive bombing…planes coming over and diving down – I don't think they realised that there was this cableway and they must have been practice runs for the Dambusters. I also remember when flares were dropped in the village overnight and there was a bomb – I think they were trying to bomb the valve shaft at the far end of the lake. They must have seen the glass roof maybe shining and he was offloading his bombs. They were in direct line with the tower but within about one hundred yards on the fellside. Quite eerie that night. Of course it could be a good target. That was the only time we ever experienced any bombing."

Bobby Eastham on leave with his mother and wife, Dorothy

Completion of the dam - dismantling the village

By 1942 water was accumulating behind the dam and the whole length of Mardale became a lake. Most of the village buildings were being dismantled keeping only the houses in the part of Burnbanks furthest from the dam. The remaining houses were retained for workers who were needed to take charge of the waterworks and general estate maintenance. Because the land owned by Manchester Corporation was held by tenant farmers, the Corporation was responsible for maintenance of the buildings, the walls and fences and the trees. So a work force of building workers, plumbers, electricians, wall builders and forestry workers was needed.

The large area between the remaining houses and the dam was fenced off and trees planted. This was where the canteen, many of the houses, the entertainment hall, and the main office had been situated.

Aerial view of completed dam with Burnbanks in the right foreground

Mrs Sharp recalls the event which was organised to celebrate the end of the dam-building and moving away of most of the workers: "There was a big farewell dance and dress-up occasion in early 1940 'Go as you please'. Everyone in the village had such a good time even though the war had started. I was thirteen and wore a party dress (long white with lace etc) and I looked adoringly at the boy Sullivan who was 18 and on his first leave from the RAF. He had too much to drink and he danced with me until my father intervened nicely! He said to me "When the war is over I will come back and ask you to marry me". He was laughing and staggering slightly and my Father led him away for a coffee. I was sent home to bed with the little ones, and I never saw him again. I only remembered recently."

FAREWELL TO BURN BANKS

Workers' Social Activities Close

The dam having been completed, Burn Banks, the village created at Haweswater by the Manchester Corporation, is gradually fading out. On the works, the dismantling of the two cableways across the valley is nearing completion and the power station is being dismantled.

The social activities of the Village came to an end on Saturday night, when both the Recreation Hall and Canteen Works Club closed down finally, the two buildings having been purchased by the Y.M.C.A. for re-erection elsewhere.

On Friday, members of the Haweswater Waterworks Club met in the canteen and spent an enjoyable evening under the auspices of the Canteen Committee. Vocal items were rendered by Messrs. Astbury, Crabtree, G. Dent, Sandham, T. Toone, Farrell, H. Toone, Cowan and Dodd, with Mr. H. Wishart, Penrith, at the piano. Mr. Dodd acted as chairman, and at the close wished Mr. W. C. Cannon (the manager) and his sisters and brother God speed and good luck in their new home. Mr. Cannon replied, saying he had made many friends during his stay in Burn Banks and hoped they would remain friends.

On Saturday afternoon, the children's sports were held. Each child received nuts (the gift of Mr. Darwin Leighton, Kendal) and a packet of sweets, the gift of the Canteen Committee, who gave £4 10s. to enable the sports to be carried out. The Recreation Hall committee had charge of the afternoon's proceedings.

The farewell dance in the Recreation Hall brought to an end the social activities. Dancing from 7 p.m. to 11 p.m. to music by Jackson's dance band was greatly enjoyed by all in the village, along with friends from the surrounding district. Near the close, the secretary, on behalf of the Recreation Committees, both past and present, expressed thanks for the support accorded to them during the past 11 years, and hoped that wherever destiny might lead them in the years that lay ahead they would enjoy good health and good luck. Mr. Jack Jackson, the band leader, expressed his appreciation of the many happy dances he and his band had enjoyed in the Hall. At the close, all joined hands and sang "Auld Lang Syne."

Cumberland Herald 26th July 1941.

Mr Rawlings tells us that some of the allotments were used for forestry as they became vacant, providing wood for estate maintenance: "When people were going away from the allotments then we commandeered about the first, from the works side, about four allotments and we grew our own spruce - Norwegian spruce, Sitka spruce, Japanese larch, I don't think we planted any larch, it was always Japanese larch because it's a very fast grower."

Arthur Cannon remembers the dam filling up: "It would probably be the summer in 1941 after scheme was finished and the water was coming over the top. There was always compensation water that went in the base of the tunnel that goes out to the River Lowther down there. That lake I would say when it set off it would only be maybe about two and a half mile in length but it finished up after it was full about four miles I would think, it holds quite a volume of water."

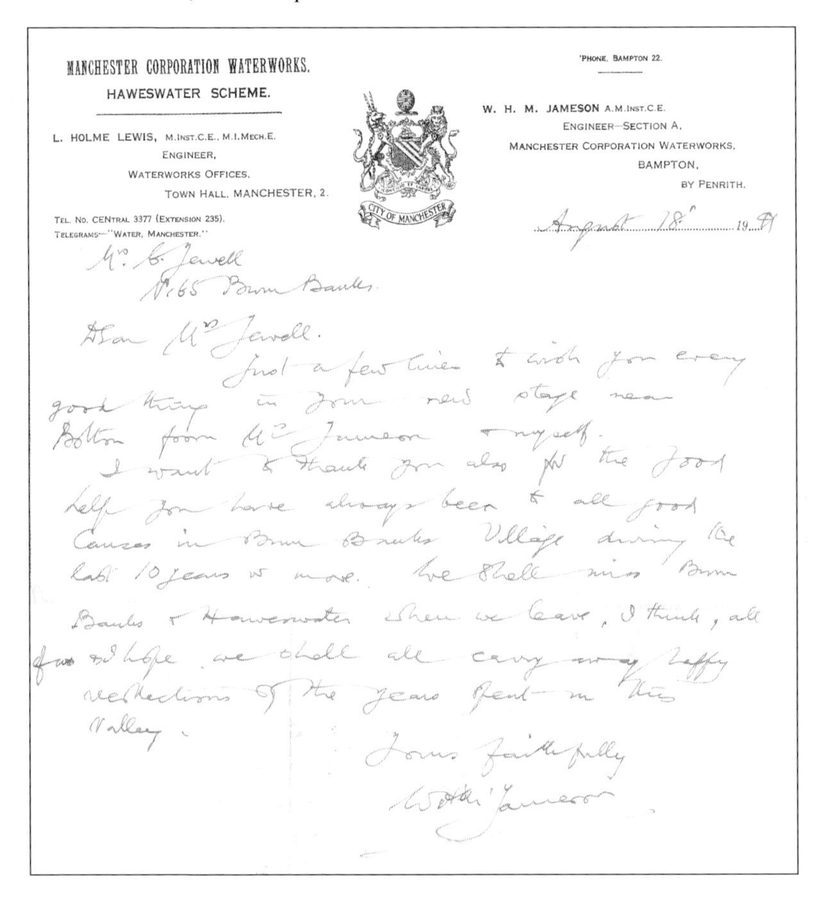

MANCHESTER CORPORATION WATERWORKS.
HAWESWATER SCHEME.

L. HOLME LEWIS, M.INST.C.E., M.I.MECH.E.
ENGINEER,
WATERWORKS OFFICES,
TOWN HALL, MANCHESTER, 2.

TEL. NO. CENTRAL 3377 (EXTENSION 235).
TELEGRAMS—"WATER, MANCHESTER."

CITY OF MANCHESTER

'PHONE, BAMPTON 22.

W. H. M. JAMESON A.M.INST.C.E.
ENGINEER—SECTION A,
MANCHESTER CORPORATION WATERWORKS,
BAMPTON,
BY PENRITH.

August 18th 1941

Mr C. Jewell
No 65 Burn Banks.

Dear Mr Jewell.

Just a few lines to wish you every good thing in your new stage near Bolton from Mrs Jameson & myself.

I want to thank you also for the good help you have always been to all good causes in Burn Banks Village during the last 10 years or more. We shall miss Burn Banks & Haweswater when we leave, I think, all of us & I hope we shall all carry many happy recollections of the years spent in this Valley.

Yours faithfully
W.H.M. Jameson

The houses and other buildings that had been dismantled were quickly taken away and re-assembled elsewhere as there was a great demand for temporary buildings during the War. Most of the ones which were sold for wartime purposes have now gone but some which were to be simply used as houses remain in Shap and a few other places. The Mission Hall is now the Village Hall at Thirlmere. It has recently been refurbished and looks very smart.

Bobby Eastham remembers taking down the houses: "And then at the tail end, I was one of the last to be called up, I helped to take some of those houses down, and they were transported all over. People bought them, and we used to take them down for them. And they were taken to Shap and went by rail, or some went by lorry. There are two at Shap village, at Shap Granite, there are two there."

Dismantling one of the huts. Back row left to right: Billy Thompson, John Texter (on leave from RAF), Ted Thompson. Front row: Henry Routledge (clerk), Tom Lucas, Walter Bracken, Bobby Eastham

Before he eventually moved to Shap, Bill Rawlings remembers the dismantling of the recreation building: "..(*the recreation building*) was pulled down. Half of the recreation (*building*) came to Barrow and it was on the prom just where you turned at the lights. It was there for years and years and years. It was a library there before it was knocked down. I remember them pulling that down actually and they took it down bit by bit. I can actually remember a man falling off the roof and he came down but it wasn't too bad - maybe broke a leg or something, you know."

Arthur Cannon recalls the sometimes dangerous nature of his own job taking down poles and cables: "I remember when the work had ceased on the dam and the village became pretty dormant, so a lot of the overhead lines that had been put up, well, they were put up prior to me starting in '37, well all that had to come down. And I remember just working on your own, with the ladder up on the pole and sawing through the overhead cable and then coming to the last cable to be cut and then sawing through it then the pole going – the fact that it had lost the tension of the cable – the pole swinging and being thrown off and fortunately landing in a heap of bushes. You don't realise how lucky you were, you could have been killed if you'd fallen on the concrete road and you hadn't realised what you were actually doing - that that pole was being held up in a vertical position due to the wire that you were cutting. Of course there were three or four conductors up there plus telephone wires - you probably had five different cables. Well all that had to be dismantled."

When in 1941 the construction of the dam was completed, Arthur's brother Colin, who was licencee of the club, received a brief letter from Manchester Corporation to say that as from that date his services would no longer be required. Arthur tells us; "There was no thank you for his service from 1934 to '41. It just said you'd have to vacate the premises. So Colin and my sister Binnie went to Bampton Grange, Grange Farm. He could have bought that farm for £600 but he was renting it.

"Binnie had married Bill Johnson, another dam project employee, and he was away serving in the Coldstream Guards then returned to Bampton Grange. Then he and Binnie took a pub themselves in Penrith. They got the tenancy for that from Glasson's brewery and they finished up they had two or three others – they had the General Wolfe. Phemie had volunteered for the RAF." So Arthur used to travel to work from Bampton Grange until he was eventually called up in 1942.

There were apparently local fears of the dam bursting. Chris Holme explains: "I was born the same year as it was flooded in 1941. So it was a new thing when I went to school from being five years old, and they always used to talk, 'what if the dam bursts?' and things like that. We always used to get each other worked up about it, but as years went by I think everybody learned to live with it and realised it wasn't going to burst."

Sent as a postcard 14th January 1948 with the words, " To my Dear Pal Joe from Freddie. Good Health and plenty of good luck."

Post war – a quiet place

For many years what remained of Burnbanks was a quiet place to live which became increasingly attractive as a great wood grew up to blot out the view of the dam and as the families had time to cultivate their gardens to a very high standard. The houses were painted and well maintained and a visitor would not guess that they were made of cast iron.

There was more work to be done to finish off the original project to create a system of weirs and pipes to divert water from Swindale Beck and Heltondale into Haweswater and later to build a small reservoir in Wet Sleddale. And all the remaining properties owned by the Corporation had to be maintained and walls and fencing kept in order. This kept some in employment and even brought new residents for a time.

The houses that had been built away from the main village for occupation by the tradesmen and managers were more desirable and some staff chose to remain after their retirement and even Alderman Walker retired to Naddlegate. Some houses were eventually sold and became valuable, sought after properties in such a scenic location.

Raymond Holliday's father continued to work in Burnbanks: "Late on in maybe about the '50s my dad got a job in charge of the stores then they moved down to the Oaks.

"I joined the ROC (Royal Observer Corps) in my teens in about 1954 which was held at Bampton I believe. So when my National Service call up papers came I was able to join the RAF, finishing in 1958."

Walter Twigg's father also continued to work at Burnbanks until the early 1950s.

Raymond Holliday on his motor bike in the 1950s outside No 1 Burnbanks

June Holliday on her wedding day outside The Oaks

June and Raymond Holliday in the garden of The Oaks in the 1950s. Some houses had already been dismantled.

A group of local girls outside the Post Office (No 2 Burnbanks) on the day of June Holliday's wedding in 1956

Ernest Hartness' Commer bus crossing the Black Bridge between Bampton and Bampton Grange

Angus and Margaret Edkins arrived at Burnbanks in 1956. He recalls: "I was an engineering assistant with Manchester waterworks at the time. Or that's the post that I went to take up. There was my wife and myself and we had one baby girl at that time. I worked in one of the houses up in the village next to the estate office. There was Sid Wear in the estate office and I was at the other end of that building. That was my office. I was employed on the new works that were being worked in Swindale. I got there towards the end of the driving of the tunnel from Swindale to Haweswater.

Above: *Bampton Clinic 1956 with Nurse McCormick*

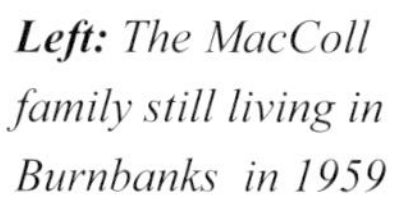

Left: *The MacColl family still living in Burnbanks in 1959*

Swindale weir 1960

"We had trouble with our house (*at Naddlegate*) from time to time. There was no insulation on the walls. It was just the weatherboarding on the outside, and Essex boarding on the inside, and nothing between them. Essex boarding is just like a kind of paperboard. It's about that (an inch) thick. Just like compressed paper more or less. The walls had all been more or less whitewashed, and if you wanted to clean them you had to be very careful because the surface used to come off it."

His wife remembers that the walls became quite spongy in the winter when drying nappies inside. Nevertheless they loved their Burnbanks home: "But they were nice little bungalows. They were nicely laid out. They were as good as they could be. We enjoyed it."

But they found the resident workers were suspicious of them as if he'd been sent by management to watch them: "I wasn't on the establishment - everybody else was part of the estates. I wasn't. I was on the new works. I think it was just as much the fact that they'd never had an engineer there before. Not nasty but a barrier nevertheless. And as I say I was shown the parlour the first time (*I went to the post office in Madge Scott's house*). Never again after that. They began to realize that we were human beings."

One neighbour who Madge Scott certainly would open up her parlour to would be Sir William Walker. He chose to live at Burnbanks when he retired from the Waterworks Committee in Manchester and Mr and Mrs Edkins remember that he had an elderly housekeeper called Penny. They recall: "Once a year, instead of sweeping the chimney of the house, Penny used to set fire to the chimney. We always knew she was spring cleaning. I was petrified because they were wooden houses at Naddlegate."

The Edkins' two daughters were both born in Burnbanks: "They were born in that front bedroom, in dreadful conditions one of them, poor child."

Mr Edkins remembers filling up with petrol at John Bowness's in Bampton and that medicines came via the milkman from Shap. During an outbreak of Asian 'flu, he recalls the doctor's advice: "Take as many (*pills*) as you need and don't come back."

He also recalls getting paid in cash by registered post and being alarmed the first time he witnessed the dam overflowing after heavy rain: "That I do remember - the first time the dam overflowed after we moved in. In the middle of the night. 'What's that noise!?' And I said, 'I'm glad we're at Naddlegate and not in the village.' Because I think it would have been quite frightening. Mind you, of course, they would have been expecting it."

Sylvia Hindmarch tells us about moving into her home at No 1 Burnbanks in 1960 with husband George, who had been brought up in the village and whose parents still lived there: "The works yard was across the road in the corner, by the garages, and that's where all the men used to start work, because there was a joiner's shop, there was a blacksmith's shop, there was a painter's shop, there was everybody, you know. And my husband, well he used to go out to the outlying farms, do repairs and that, alterations and building work. There was also a time keeper over there where they had to clock in and clock out of a night. And then there was the man that lived next door, Tim Scott, he used to go up to the dam and look after that and see everything was alright in there because there used to be a lot of things in the dam in them days.

"..everybody lived in the village you see: the painters and decorators, the plumbers and the joiners they all lived in the village. But they went out onto the farms and various places and anything that belonged to the Manchester Corporation they used to go and maintain it in those days.. The blacksmith of course was Audrey Parkin's dad, Alec Little, he did bike up from Bampton. He didn't live in the village. And you see my husband he was on the building side then he went over onto the water side for a little while and he used to get transport down to Bampton and then he used to go through (*and along*) a footpath that goes through by Rheda Brennand's just at Conn Cottage there, and it used to go up the Howes to Cawdale because there's a little water house up there. He used to look after that and then he used to go through the water line right through to Heltondale and keep all the gutters clean so that it kept the water running."

George used to go after he had finished work to help Sylvia's aunt and uncle who farmed at Knipe Hall particularly at hay timing. Sylvia tells us that the working day at Burnbanks was from eight o'clock till half past four and wages possibly about £10 a week when they first arrived. The rent for their house was about 11 shillings.

George and Olive Hindmarch in 1972, outside their Burnbanks home

She paints a happy picture of life in Burnbanks around that time: "When we moved to Burnbanks sixteen houses were occupied, all by Manchester Corporation Water Works employees. Where the houses had been removed there was just a concrete foundation, just bare: the children of the village used to play football and also rode their bikes on them. Also over the cattle grid up the village where the tennis courts and bowling green were it was bare. Now trees have been planted on that site. In the village itself the trees were not very tall and there weren't as many as there are today - a lot of the trees have grown from seedlings. There were no garages as there weren't many cars - George's Dad built those (*the original garages*). The road was kept in quite good repair. In winter when we had snow all the workmen turned out with shovels to clear the village so that the retailers got through with milk, bread etc and also the workmen.

"We were well looked after by MCWW (Manchester Corporation Waterworks). We were even delivered with free loads of logs for our fires. Also dustbins were emptied every week. There was a village rubbish dump below the dam. The road up the back went right round the village, past the stores, so didn't go onto the fell like today.

"There was nothing, just houses, except we had a post office next door but only a post office, nothing else, no sweeties or anything. She probably sold a few cigarettes maybe but that was all. But we were well looked after with mobile shops, butchers…There was Norman Douglas from Penrith and there was Bill Hudson used to come from Helton. He had a mobile shop selling groceries, and he used to carry bread as well. We used to get the Co-op milk van coming from Shap and in those days we used to buy little plastic discs and we bought them in little packets on a Saturday and we used to put them out every day for our milk and that was like our payment rather than putting out cash every day. We had a butcher, yes, that was Jackson's from Penrith. We also had a man came round selling shoes, from Pearson's shoe shop in Penrith. They used to come round with a vanload of shoes and you could buy shoes and slippers. There was … Henry Fairer from Shap. He used to come round with clothes, cases with clothes in them for kids and grown ups and that, and he had quite a good little shop up at Shap. And the coalman came - Taylor's from Penrith, and he came on the 15th of every month and never missed. Our coalman still comes and he's not far away from the 15th and he still comes every month which is good really."

Delivery vans eventually became less profitable as people's shopping habits changed, although the Shap Co-op continued to deliver to outlying areas.

Rosemary Thompson, who lives in Bampton, had spent a lot of time at her grandmother's (*Mrs Satterthwaite's*) at Walmgate Head, and her husband Thomas, who was brought up at Eastward, a farm near Burnbanks, both remember popping into the post office at Burnbanks and they remember Madge Scott, the postmistress. Rosemary describes her: “She had a roundish, wrinkled face but always looked contented. We went there for stamps or to post letters. You went up the steps at the side near where the phone box was and in through her back door. There was just a little counter.”

Two good friends Madge Scott and Olive Hindmarch photographed for a 1978 feature about Burnbanks, published by the North West Water Authority in-house newspaper, ‘Waterfront’

The chapel at Bampton figured strongly in people’s lives when Sylvia and George were bringing up their young family: “We (*mothers*) used to walk to chapel with all our kids. Everybody used to be going to chapel rather than church in those days. As I say it was a thriving community. And we always used to go to Morecambe once a year on the school trips and when we set off from here it used to be pouring down and we got over Shap Fell and it was lovely and sunny and take our picnics with us and it was always Morecambe, once a year. Mr Longmire and Mrs Longmire that lived in the bungalow up at Lake View, they used to go to the chapel and they were - well, if it hadn’t been for them I think it would’ve gone down a long time since. Yes we used to go and help on a Saturday night when they used to have singers and have a supper and it always used to be full house. We used to bake and make things and take them down. It was all given voluntary, all the food and quite a lot of people from up here (would attend) And of course there was the (Bampton) WI as well which started in 1932 and a lot of people from up here, the women, they went to the WI as well.”

Responsibility for Haweswater and Burnbanks passed from MCWW to North West Water then latterly to United Utilities. Maintenance of the properties apparently deteriorated in the process. The previous tenants of No 1, Hughie and Audrey Parkin, had the old fire range taken out and Manchester Corporation put in a modern tiled fireplace for which they had to pay, on top of their rent. Sylvia, who was still living in the original No 1 Burnbanks at the time of the interview, explains: “About sixpence a week I think on the rent and that was ongoing for years - it really never stopped because by the time they bought the fire grate and paid for the labour…you were paying and paying and paying on your rent so it (the loan) really didn’t often come to an end. We got our own central heating put in about eleven years ago because we just felt that we needed extra warmth. So we got in touch with the water board so see if they would come to some terms with us - we paid half and they paid half, or whatever. They said to see Mr whoever the maintenance man was, when he comes round and have a word with him. So this man came round and we had a word with him, and he said, ‘Oh it has nothing to do with me, get back in touch with the office.’ So of course my husband said, ‘I can’t be bothered with this. We’ll just put our own in.’ So we got it in the sitting room and one in each bedroom, also, and the back kitchen, but even though the radiator is turned right up we still have to light the open fire with the heat rising and the height of the ceilings.”

She also explains that the houses did not have proper foundations because they were only meant to be temporary and eventually to be dismantled. So the foundations moved over time because of the weight of the cast iron leaving gaps and cracks, and some of the wooden floors rotted and had to be replaced with solid flooring. Soundproofing also was not up to standard: "You could hear such as if we were in this front bedroom here and the people were in the next bedroom there you could hear each other talking or you could talk through the walls. As I say George's mum and the next door neighbour, they used to sit on the toilet and talk to each other through the wall. Or you could hear people coughing or if anybody lived next door and they had loud music or whatever you could hear right through."

She continues with her picture of Burnbanks life: "Oh yes, people were very friendly up here. I mean in those days you could leave your door open and wander up the village and have a chat to your neighbours and of course mother-in-law across the road every afternoon she just used to lock her back door and wander across and sit out here with Mrs Scott next door and have a couple of hours of chinwag and any passing people, you know, they used to stop and say hello and probably have a cup of tea. Then I often used to wander up the village to Mrs Dawson, who was Louie Eastham then before she married Joe Dawson and I used to go and crack (*chat*) to her because she was rather blind. I used to go and spend a little bit of time with her because she lived on her own. And then there was the Buckles that lived up the village. I used to go and see Mr and Mrs Buckle. They were elderly people, of course they moved from Swindale, they retired from farming and they came up here to live in the '60s. And of course there was Mrs Holliday across the road there, No 2 The Oaks, she was cook at Bampton school. She would start in 1957 and she cooked at school for 24 years and biked every day to school."

Sylvia herself also worked as a cook at Bampton school from 1969 until she retired 22 years later. She tells us: "When I first started there, there were about 58 kids. Of course there were quite a lot living up here then. All the houses were full of children, so it was quite a busy little community up here."

Ultimately it was decided that all the estate department workers should be pensioned off if they were near retirement age or found work with the Authority elsewhere if they were younger and their jobs would be done by sub-contract firms. Some of the retired workers remained in their houses but eventually they began to leave and their houses mostly remained empty.

Mrs Hindmarch recalls the gradual decline of the Burnbanks community: "When the jobs and that finished up here it all went to contractors, so of course (the workers) moved away to other jobs and there were fewer and fewer people. And you see such as the Haweswater Hotel, well they had a man up here that used to transport all the staff from Shap by Landrover and take the maids and the daily workers and transport them from Shap up to the hotel. He used to just transport people about. Anyway he died and his wife was able to stay in the village. Anybody that passed away - the wives or the husbands weren't pushed out of their houses, they were able to stay in but once the widows or the widowers died they didn't re-let the houses. They just let them go down which was a shame really."

Sylvia Hindmarch was still living in No 1 Burnbanks until redevelopment

Sylvia's garden in 1998

The Oaks before redevelopment in 2005

Margaret and John Pearson moved into 62 Burnbanks in October 1970 when Margaret was appointed teacher at Bampton school. She tells us: "We were made to feel very welcome by the people already living there and we went on over the years to make some very firm and long-lasting friendships.

"(*The houses were)* prefabs and they looked a little bit short of paint and that sort of thing on the outside. I think I made a bit of a fuss about the outside paint! It was a good house (*but)* it did take a bit of getting used to as it was on the chilly side because there wasn't a lot of insulation but it was all right and we soon got used to it really. From what I can remember it all seemed to be quite well maintained and the gardens were looked after mainly.

"There was quite a lot of works traffic then because of course it was a working yard. So there were vehicles of all types really. They'd be backwards and forwards – landrovers and smaller vans and large ones and all the houses had at least one car, I would think. It was a huge workforce. And some of the workforce were transported to other places to work - they weren't just working at the dam or up by the lake. A lot of people, like George Hindmarch, would be out on the fells doing different things. But a lot of them were taken to Watchgate and Thirlmere and working in the forests. I would think that we were quite unusual in that neither of us worked for North West Water. And I think we were probably the only family that didn't – I think everybody else would have some sort of a connection with working for the waterworks.

"Well, John and I were just newly married, because we were married in October 1970, so that was our first house. And Helen was born in September '73. So there were just the three of us there when Helen came, until we moved into Penrith in February '77. We were quite sorry to leave but we felt that (*buying our own house*) was what we needed to do at the time.

"The bathroom was a really peculiar shape – it was cut across the corner – I'd never seen a bathroom like that before and it was very cold – you wouldn't linger in there. And at the end of the passage was the kitchen and I think we would've had an electric cooker. At that time it was traditional I think to buy electrical goods through the electricity board and you would buy cookers and heaters and that sort of thing. You would buy them and then pay for them on your electricity bill at the end of every quarter or whatever it was, you'd pay a bit off and that's what we did.

"We had an open fire, but it didn't heat any radiators or anything. I don't think it heated the water, I don't think there was a back boiler in it – no I'm sure there was just an open fire and so we would have an immersion heater and then we had oil-fired plug-in radiators in each of the rooms as back up - particularly in the bedrooms because they were very cold. It was just something we just got used to I suppose over time.

"At that time, we lived behind Sylvia and George Hindmarch and Sylvia's mother-in-law lived opposite there and round about that time Sylvia's father-in-law died and we asked Nana, every body called her Nana Hindmarch, (*to help*) out a little bit with Helen. She started doing some work in the house because I did find it quite challenging to have a husband on shifts and a baby and a full time job and all the rest of it. Helen has never forgotten going to Nana Hindmarch's and having lemon cheese on bread.

"Mr Aynsley was the head then, and when I first came to Bampton there would be about 36 children in the school. I think 16 of them would be infants and 20 of them would be juniors. I would work with him another seven years before he retired. I would think altogether counting the secondary age children there would be probably 12 or 16 children at that time living up there (*at Burnbanks*). Some of the younger Burnbanks mums converted one of the disused houses into a little playgroup where they would collect some toys and just have a meeting place away from their houses.

"We always felt at home right from the start and we always felt as if, you know, we knew everybody and we'd have a chat with anybody that we saw and there was never a lack of community spirit."

Some threat to the peace and quiet of the village came and went in the 1970s when a plan to raise the height of the dam and another to develop the reservoir for recreational purposes were both proposed, met with fierce local opposition and were eventually abandoned. A proposal to raise smolts at a site at the foot of the dam was, however, successful and the fish farm continues to this day despite some disruption and nuisance caused by transporting large tanks of fish on heavy lorries.

Red deer stag

All that was left of Burnbanks village before redevelopment

Golden Eagle

The eagle has landed!

Most activity at Burnbanks in recent years has been due to the arrival of England's only breeding pair of golden eagles in 1969. Consequently Burnbanks became the base for a scheme to protect the eagles and subsequently an RSPB nature reserve.

Dave Shackleton came to Burnbanks in 1984 as a volunteer to work on the Eagle Protection Scheme. He tells us that eagles first nested in 1969 and that there was a protection scheme running from 1970 with a team of volunteer and paid staff, who used to stay originally at the Haweswater Hotel and then in a caravan below the dam in Burnbanks. Around the late 70s they moved into one of the Burnbanks buildings at the entrance to the depot. He recalls: "The houses opposite the entrance there, one of them had an old red cedar outside it, that was called the old offices I believe and I think we were in there for one or two years. Well when I first went to stay in number 64, it was pretty basic. There were no beds, just mattresses on the floor and because we worked a sort of shift system on the eagles, sleeping up over night, you didn't have your own mattress, you just swapped them round as they became available. Very very basic - there was no heating except an open fire. There were actually fireplaces in all the bedrooms but the only one by that time that worked was the living room. And we burned wood that we scavenged in the vicinity basically.

"There was a kitchen; a little sort of utility type storage place next to the toilet in the back. There was nowhere in number 64 to park a car really. We used to cram one outside the front of the track going up on to the fell but we had very little parking space. But in those days it wasn't an RSPB reserve at that time so it was purely protection of the eagles, running from the last week in March through to the end of July. I think there were three paid staff by then and up to three volunteers a week coming from all over the country.

"It was cold. When I arrived it was very cold but 1984 was an extremely hot summer and it became very hot. Subsequently when we were in there all year round they were very cold in the winter and very hot in the summer with very high ceilings. From what I remember 64 wasn't in particularly good condition. Some of the cladding was falling off the outside at that time and you could see that the walls were bowed under the weight of the ceiling by then. And the doorframes didn't fit - they'd all bowed as well.

"When I came there were the Harrisons, he was the reservoir keeper, and there was Raymond the assistant, there was George and Sylvia Hindmarch, Norman Buckle and family, Keith and Gina Harrison on the end - I think George and Sylvia's son was still in the village and Judy whose surname I don't know she was in the village as well and Madge Scott and Nana Hindmarch - oh and Mrs Walker and Jack Buckle and his brother who I think was called Cliff - so in fact they were probably almost all occupied apart from the one opposite the entrance to the depot - the old offices I think, and 63 wasn't occupied next door to us. The rest of them may well have all been occupied at that time. But when I came here there were no community institutions left, everything had gone, there was just the houses and nothing else.

"Round about 1987 we moved into No. 62. We were never in 63 - that was always empty I think, which is just an identical building. And then we slowly took over 61 as well. Well it was unoccupied and we had a lot of volunteers, and the Water Authority let us use that one as well. I can't remember what year it was but they replaced all the windows in the front – round about 1990 I think.

"One other thing that we used to have to do when new volunteers arrived: there was always a suspicion that there was a possibility that the dam could be a terrorist target, particularly when the troubles in Northern Ireland were at their height. So any new volunteers we had to take down to introduce to the reservoir keeper or his assistant and they were given a briefing and we all had permits in those days. And we weren't allowed between the depot and the dam, we weren't even allowed to go there when I first came here. We were allowed to use the concrete road and that's really what the permits were for, but that was it.

"It became an RSPB Reserve in the spring of 1988 and the whole operation became on a much grander scale then. We had a permanent member of staff here all year round, plus three summer contract wardens. We also had many more volunteers, not just working on the eagles but also on survey work and management. So at any one time in numbers 61 and 62 there might have been ten to fifteen people staying, when it was very busy. So it was quite cramped and again very basic, just the heaters in the living rooms, or the open fires. Actually, 62 was in quite good condition and 61 had been lived in until quite recently by Raymond Crabtree who then moved into the new house next door up the hill. So they were in a lot better condition than 64 was. The ceilings hadn't been lowered like they had in some of them. I think they had just been looked after better by the people who had lived in them. The kitchen was fairly modernised in 62 from what I remember.

"We established the tree nursery around about 1990. When we took it over it was full of Christmas trees that were only a couple of years old really and over the next three or four years we eventually got rid of all those, we ploughed it and made raised beds in it. Prior to that it had been a paddock for a horse which had been owned by Barbara Harrison, the wife of the previous reservoir keeper and prior to that I think it had been tennis courts - I'm not sure. So the tree nursery has produced a lot of trees over the years for the surrounding area, mostly oak trees, a few junipers now and probably half our volunteer time is spent in the tree nursery still, although we are not actually living in the village anymore. We also had a workshop in the barn which is being converted at Thornthwaite Mill and then we moved the workshop into one of the old buildings in the depot - that would have been about ten years ago now. So we've got a workshop down there as well and we store some equipment there and all the odd jobs are done there like any woodworking type things. But we don't have electricity so there's no power saws or anything like that.

"When I first came it was North West Water now United Utilities - we have always had a good relationship with them and now they actually pay the wages of the eagle warden through the summer. And they supply us with a lot of the materials that we use for fencing and things like that … and in return we deliver some of their biodiversity objectives.

"The other big thing I guess that has happened is the arrival of the fish farm, about privatisation time I think. This has increased a lot of the traffic through the village and that area below the dam obviously is much more disturbed than it ever once was. It was a real wildlife haven, one of the few of the least disturbed places in the whole Lake District probably because it was all strictly private. But with the fish farm coming and various other developments there's more activity under there now.

"There's a nice alder-dominated woodland community which is quite unusual in the Lake District really, the sort of wet woodlandy bit. There are some very old oaks. There are some nice lichen epiphyte communities actually on the trees. And there's kingfishers, well kingfishers don't breed there but they winter there."

Although David didn't mention red squirrels, Burnbanks sustains a healthy population of these endangered mammals. Sylvia Hindmarch has been a leading figure in the local campaign to preserve them in the valley. When we interviwed Sylvia and George in their old bungalow for the Bampton book, red squirrels were feeding right in front of their window, which was quite a distraction!

Deterioration of no 63 and 64 Burnbanks, 2005

No 61 and 62, partly modernised for RSPB

No 9 and 10 Burnbanks 1998

George and Sylvia receiving visitors, the Jewell family at No 1 Burnbanks in 1998

No 66 Burnbanks, the Jewells lived at 65 next door, in 1998

Redevelopment – Burnbanks reborn

No community is anything without the people – it's not the bricks and mortar, it's the people and you're treading on those people's lives and memories and histories.

Nick Paxman, developer

The original plan had been for the village to be demolished and the land put back to its original state but Burnbanks had become part of the Bampton community where there was an urgent need for affordable housing. So various efforts were made over recent years to redevelop the village. But eventually only two houses remained occupied, residents moving out often because of the uncertain future of Burnbanks or the deterioration of their homes. And because of the very poor insulation and ventilation, the unoccupied houses deteriorated very rapidly.

Rear view of 1 and 2 The Oaks prior to redevelopment

A Burnbanks house abandoned and forlorn

All that's left of the mission hall

The Oaks being dismantled 2005

Foundations that were the canteen and recreation hall

Old garages at Burnbanks, now dismantled and rebuilt

After several years of negotiations with the planning authorities a private firm eventually bought all the houses. Plans were drawn up to build new dwellings, with local occupancy restrictions, on the same sites as the old ones and of similar dimensions but using modern materials and to acceptable modern standards.

Nick Paxman is a director of Ocala Construction, the developers undertaking the redevelopment and rebuilding of the Burnbanks village. Apparently he and his fellow director Trevor Ingram, instantly fell in love with the site after seeing it advertised then coming to view it. And at that time Nick was unaware of a family historical connection with Burnbanks. But it transpired that his wife's family lived at Knipe and her Aunt Madge kept the post office at Burnbanks and lived out her days there at number 2.

It took Ocala about three years to get through the legal and environmental stages of the development and work eventually began on site on the 1st May, 2004. Much of the original village, demolished long ago, was not included in the development site, though remains of it can still be spotted round about.

First of all Ocala demolished the remaining properties providing an insight into their construction. Nick Paxman describes them thus: "They're a cast iron, pre-fabricated construction of which I've never seen anything like it anywhere else. I've spent twenty five years of my working life entirely in property throughout the North-West in a general practice, chartered surveyor role, in the last ten years in property development, and although I've come across umpteen different sorts of concrete pre-fabricated designs, the majority dating from just after the war when the building material shortage was on, I've never seen any built of cast iron before.

"They were very much a kit form construction. Each of the panels in the properties were numbered and from what we've been able to discover there were different shaped pieces numbered B1 through to B7 and that seems to be the only seven pieces that were used in any of the different properties, whether they were the semi-detached ones or whether they were the office buildings in the works yard. They covered all the different shapes that you had in a wall, in a corner post, above and below a window and over a door head with seven different pieces. I suppose if you think of Lego you can similarly build any sort of house or car or castle out of probably no more that seven different sized pieces of Lego, so the principle was probably an easy one to follow.

Cast iron panel and fibreboard wall revealed

Panels after demolition

"Those cast iron panels were just bolted together with iron bolts – quite amazing in that I think it probably shows how the walls of the properties kept the damp out. We were actually able to undo the bolts in probably ninety nine percent of the cases, having sat there in the wall for seventy five years, or whatever it is, and they hadn't corroded to any point that they wouldn't just come off with an air line and a spanner on the end.

"They were built with basically no foundations. The base of the properties was an iron girder frame, a normal H-section girder - an RSJ, or a universal beam - laid on the ground and the bottom panels were just bolted into that girder. If you looked around the majority of the properties the external walls were beginning to bow ever so slightly. You could see this down the sides of the door frames and where the internal partitions join the outside walls you could see that all of them were suffering the same sort of fatigue and the front walls were very gradually becoming the shape of a banana, due to the fact that this girder they were on was just corroding away so it was beginning to sag under the weight of the cast iron which was just sat on the ground. In one or two places where they'd contoured the ground slightly there was a concrete pile in each corner of the building. None of them were more than a couple of feet deep – so nowhere did they have anything that would constitute a proper foundation. The floor was then just laid between these iron girders on a very shallow layer of gravel. The floors under the wet rooms – under the bathroom, the kitchen and the pantries – were done in solid concrete. The rest of the floors were a timber floor but those timber joists were just sat on top of this very thin layer of gravel and they were all very badly rotten and in one or two of the properties you could see where some repairs had been done over the years because the floorboards were getting a bit rotten.

"The roofs were a traditional timber rafter roof covered with a light weight asbestos cement tile. The whole of the roof was then covered with four or five-by-one timber - in proper building terms it was put on as a sarking board then light-weight tiles nailed on top of it. It gives you a bit more protection from the rain when it comes in, so you can take the tiles off and you've still got a solid timber roof.

"Because the construction internally was very flimsy, there was no plaster work, no plasterboard, no plastering of any description within the properties. The inside lining of the cast iron was a very thin fibreboard. In the larger square cast iron panels there was a square in the middle where a chock of wood was banged in and then a fairly small timber stud was nailed on to that and then this fibre board was just nailed over the top of it. The insulation qualities were absolutely zero so they must have been perishing cold in the winter and potentially, particularly where the fronts were facing south, they must have warmed up like a storage heater in the summer with the heat getting absorbed by the cast iron and staying there for quite some time.

"When we stripped the asbestos tiles off the roof there was evidence that a lot of them had wood burning stoves with stove chimneys sticking out through the roof because there were lots of little round holes in the timber sarking which had been covered over. In the original properties they probably had a lot of little pot bellied stoves with stove pipes and at some time later they've added the chimney stacks – which were built in Whitehaven red brick. When we knocked them down they've got Whitehaven stamped through them like Blackpool rock.

"When we started the demolition the wood was unfortunately not recyclable from our point of view in building, so we did start burning quite a lot of the timber initially. And then one person would come along and ask if they could have a few bits so (*gradually*) more and more local people appeared with trailers, and quite a lot of it did get taken away. Now I know some farmers

The China Connection!

The cast iron panels – I did my best to ensure we kept an intact one of each piece to go to the history society. The rest disappeared off in wagons and in the way of the world at the moment it all went by sea to fuel China's booming economy, being the place most scrap is now heading to as we can't keep up with the production. All the rest of them went by road down to Liverpool docks and then disappeared off to China.

Nick Paxman

have reused it into making sheep rails and sheep pens. I know some's gone into people's gardens and the RSPB have used it for relining beds and borders of the tree nursery.

"A couple of the properties still had the old solid fuel fired boiler, that people would have done their washing in - the big iron pots – can't think what the proper name is. We did try in two properties to recover one intact for the history society, but they were cast iron as well and they were very well built into the brickwork around them. We got one out still encased in a load of brick but in trying to chisel the bricks off then that one broke as well so I'm afraid we failed on that. The surviving properties that were still occupied had variously had new domestic hot water systems put in. They had modern copper hot water cylinders and electric immersions. A couple of them had had fairly recent bathrooms put in but the vast majority were still the original cast iron bath and high level suite in the WC.

"There had been very little other modernisation done really. Those slightly newer ones had been electrically rewired. The one or two pairs that were here when we came along that had been empty for many years they still had the remnants of Wyrelex wiring in. Originally it would have been the Wyrelex - the three straight pins, and the cabling was either lead-covered or cloth-covered. It was two square pins and the little red pin in the middle. But otherwise, I don't think particularly the water board had ever seen fit to spend very much money on them at all.

"The only other main part of the village in the development that we've had a big building involvement in has been replacing the whole of the drainage system. The drainage system, for its age, was not unusual but the foul water and the surface water all went down the same pipe which went into a clinker bed rotating treatment plant, down in the woods behind The Oaks. What must always have been a problem with that was when it rained very heavily and you get a surge of top-water coming off all the roofs. The disposal in the soak-away would only cope with a trickle of water so when it rained heavily it must always have caused some degree of pollution. It was probably good that there's only been a few people living here for the last number of years, otherwise the state of it would have been somewhat worse. We now have a separate foul drainage system and one of the new Bio-Disk package treatment plants. And we've put a reed-bed in behind that as well. So it's now a very clean system and in another year or two it will be a very good wildlife habitat in itself."

Steel girders and square cast iron panels making Burnbanks houses in January 1930

And with the demolition of the buildings and the building of the new ones a number of bat habitats were surveyed in the area and several species of bats roost in and around the village as well. It truly is a very beautiful, rich wildlife habitat here.

"What people see now as a village within a wood, wasn't in fact a wood originally. The conifer plantation between here and the dam was all planted by the water board as landscaping to shield the front of the dam from view from afar. A lot of the woodland around the area of the village that we've been developing is just self-seeded native aforestation. The big stand of Scots pine that ran across the back of the village behind 54 down to 66 was I'm told planted by the water board in relatively recent times. Burnbanks wasn't a wood in early days – it was just open countryside."

Demolition

Nick Paxman concludes: "Trevor and I feel honoured to have been a part of that transformation - to come into a still-living community, an entire village, and recreate it and rebuild. It makes you also very sensitive and aware of what the village has meant to so many people and how it has been a community - how it's been a lifelong home for some people. One of the tenants that was living here when we first started work had been here from

A new Burnbanks is born

1929 as a six month old baby and we come along and in a very short length of time, a two or two and a half year period, we'll have started and finished the redevelopment of the village and that's just a blink of the eye in the lifetime of the people who have been Burnbanks and have been the village.

"No community is anything without the people – it's not the bricks and mortar, it's the people and you're treading on those people's lives and memories and histories. We hope we've been sympathetic to that. It does really have deep meaning to us, to have done such a very unusual development project."

Pat Garside, Bob Dickman and Nick Paxman with the Rt Hon David Maclean MP unveiling the commemorative plaque at Burnbanks 2006

Maighread Sharp with Sylvia Hindmarch 2006

Panels and artefacts on display at Manchester Central Reference Library during the Burnbanks Exhibition

Some former residents have revisited Burnbanks, including those who travelled from far and wide for the official opening of the 'new' village by local MP David Maclean in 2006. Mairghread Sharp, when she wrote to us from Australia, told us that she had returned to Burnbanks in 2000 (she also visited in 2006). She wrote: "I often do not remember what I was doing yesterday but I can still see and hear most of the people who lived in Burnbanks between 1933 and 1940.. … I returned in 2000 to look at the remains of the houses and it was grey and dingy – very gloomy. But as I walked up the front road past the football field I could hear the voices and name all of them – boys I went to school with, some lost in World War Two."

Margaret Higson visited in Spring 2004, 60 years after her family left. She wrote after her visit: "The ridge tiles of numbers 1 and 2 The Oaks were being removed. A few bats were recovered. It is sad to see the village now but I believe it will be a community again when the new bungalows are built. I would like to think they will be people who know the area and will bring life back to the village. While I was there I could imagine the people and places of the past. We were very fortunate children."

Sylvia Hindmarch still at No 1!

Acknowledgements

This book draws on research conducted by the Bampton and District Local History Society (BDLHS) over a period of three years from 2003 to 2006. It was inspired by John Drinkwater whose 'self-sufficient' life at the head of Swindale had made him a frequenter of the streams, habitations and woodlands around Mardale. Knowing how much of Burnbanks had already been lost among saplings and scrub, John directed the attention of the newly formed BDLHS to the significance of the dwindling village and suggested that recovering its history would be a valuable project.

Burnbanks has been a mammoth project for a very small parish – all told, around 50% of our residents have taken an active part in it over a sustained period of three years. It has been a supreme effort of sharing, valuing and mutual enjoyment. Throughout, the Burnbanks steering group of the BDLHS has successfully maintained the necessary momentum and cohesion - many thanks to this remarkable team: Bob Dickman, Helen Farrow, John and Marion Drinkwater, Chris Wood, Liz Hall, Caz Walker and Sharron Metcalfe.

Local history also needs to be seen and heard – with our Local Heritage Initiative grant, we undertook to stage exhibitions, to design and mount an interpretative panel at Burnbanks, to make a digital photographic archive, a website, an oral archive and to stage a pantomime based on historic events at the dam and village. That seemed quite enough but ultimately producing a book proved irresistible and we were awarded an extended and enhanced LHI grant to do this. We felt we had the material to successfully complete all these tasks thanks to the excellent work of our production team: Dennis and Chris at Fullpoint; Vicky and her team at Eden Graphics; Dean Marshall and his team at Reed's Printers; Sharron Metcalfe who took responsibility for the digital archive; Caz Walker who led the oral history exercise, and her fellow interviewers, Maureen Cummings, Bob Dickman, and Christine Gillespie; Liz Hall, Alison Jones and all their panto helpers; John Garside for his timeline, Malcolm Evans for his scale models and Tony Smith for his scale drawings; Trevor Ingram and Nick Paxman of Ocala Property Development whose enthusiasm for the old Burnbanks proved as great as their belief in its regeneration; and Chris Cant who set up the website www.bampton-history.org.uk where much of our material, including sound recordings, photos and transcriptions, can be accessed at the click of a mouse.

To gather material for the book, and especially to try and track down people who had memories of Burnbanks, we held a series of open days and exhibitions. We would especially like to thank librarians and archivists at Penrith Museum, Kendal Local Studies Centre, and Manchester Central Reference Library and in particular Judith Clarke and Sidney Chapman (Penrith), Jacky Fay and Hester Gorman (Kendal) and Steve Willis (Manchester). They enthusiastically provided us with a fascinating range of venues to display our findings. They added to our material and improved our understanding, and helped us to keep track of people who visited the exhibitions and who could help us further. James Cropper, Lord Lieutenant of Cumbria, was generous enough to open our Kendal exhibition and our local MP, the Rt Hon David Maclean, came to unveil our commemorative plaque at Burnbanks and wrote a foreward for this book.

We are especially grateful to the Local Heritage Initiative (LHI), the Heritage Lottery Fund, Nationwide Building Society and the Countryside Agency for financial and organisational support in the initial stages of the project and for more recent support in the production of this book. Susannah England and Gillian Woodcock of the Countryside Agency were model mentors – encouraging, challenging and professional, expecting the highest standards in the conduct of the research while putting us in touch with specialist advisors to assist us. We especially valued the contribution of Roger Kitchen, LHI Project Support Worker, in setting up the Burnbanks Digital Archive and of Ian McNicol, Artistic Advisor to the Burnbanks Pantomime 'A Lad in Burnbanks'. Of course we also have to thank all our local thespians and helpers who made that show such a memorable occasion.

At the heart of the Burnbanks exhibitions were historic images of the Haweswater dam operation and the village of Burnbanks itself. Some of these came from organisations that had been involved and in particular Manchester City Council (Manchester Archives and Local Studies Digital Collection), The Lake District National Park Archaeology Unit and United Utilities. The people who guided us through their rich collections included Eleanor Kingston and Andy Lowe (LDNP), Dave Bury, Edward Holt and Martin Moorby, (UU). Other material came from a small band of tireless local historians, especially Jean Jackson and John Graham of Shap and John Cooke of Liverpool.

This book might never have been written without the willingness of others to voluntarily share their expertise. We were particularly helped by discussions with the North West Sound Archive, Burneside Heritage Group, the Ambleside Oral History Group and the Shap, Crosby Ravensworth and Sedbergh Local History Societies. We also gained a great advantage through Jane Gregg's expertise and fresh eye, which rekindled everyone's determination to see the history of Burnbanks in print and who transformed our archive of pictures, interviews and documents into a publishable entity.

Last but by no means least, special thanks are due to all those individuals who gave freely of their private collections. These include Arthur Cannon (Carlisle) the late Delwyn Davies (Cheshire) Mr and Mrs Hughie Davins (Bury) the Eastham family (Lancaster) Angus and Margaret Edkins (Warrington) Margaret and Peter Higson (Stoke-on-Trent) Fay Howard and Robert Gibb (Manchester) Ray Holliday (Penruddock) Betty and Eric Jewell and family (Bolton) June Nanson and Joyce Arran (Northampton) Jean Newhouse (Milnthorpe) the MacColl family (Australia) Thomas Moore (Penrith) Marjorie Ord (Clitheroe) Bill Rawlings, the Slessor family (Penrith) and Walter Twigg (Carlisle). Closer to home we have to thank Sylvia Hindmarch, Chris Holme, Audrey Parkin, Margaret Pearson and David Shackleton, John Thompson and George Brunskill. To them all - thank you for taking us on an engrossing tour of Haweswater and Burnbanks!

Pat Garside, BDLHS Burnbanks Project Coordinator.

Do You Know That ..... ?

1. The name Haweswater probably comes for the Norse Hafr's water. This could be a Norse personal name or the Old Norse for 'goat'.

2. Haweswater dam is 30 metres (96 feet) high and 470 metres (1550 feet) long. The safe reliable yield from the Haweswater scheme is 66 million gallons (about 300,000 cubic metres) of water a day. The draw-off tower stands on the shore about half-a-mile south of the Haweswater Hotel.

3. Alderman William Walker, Chairman of the Manchester Waterworks Committee in the 1930s, retired to Naddlegate, Burnbanks where he died in 1961, aged 93.

4. When full, the surface of Haweswater is about 240 metres (790ft) above sea level. Water from Haweswater flows 'downhill' to Manchester without the need for any pumps on the way.

5. Before the valley of Mardale was flooded, the natural Hawes Water was the highest of the main lakes. It was about 4 km (2½ miles) long and almost divided into two parts at Measand Beck. The smaller eastern end was known as Low Water and the end beyond Measand as High Water. The Kitchen family rowed a ferry across the narrow strait.

6. In 1972 a proposal was made to raise the height of the dam to about 70 metres (230 feet), increasing its capacity to 65 thousand million gallons (290 million cubic metres).

7. The Earls of Lonsdale retained the fishing rights to Haweswater. Trout and char were caught for the Lonsdale table. Today trout, perch and pike can still be found.

8. At the entrance to Burnbanks village there used to be gates that were locked at night to keep the residents in (and intruders out?)

9. The lych gates at Bampton Parish Church were made in the workshop at Burnbanks and presented by Manchester City Corporation as a 'thank you' for putting up with the disruption caused by the building of the dam.

10. The capacity of Haweswater is almost 19 thousand million gallons (about 85 million cubic metres). This is enough to provide every man, woman and child in the UK with almost 8000 cups of tea, enough to keep us all going for about 7 years!

11. A resident of Burnbanks who now lives in Sydney, Australia, has called her house 'Burnbanks'.

12. One of the first babies born in the village of Burnbanks was named Irene Burnbanks Thompson.

A LAD IN BURNBANKS

The cast of the Bampton play, A Lad in Burnbanks, which is being performed at the village hall this weekend. The show presents the findings of a Bampton and District Local History Society research project into Burnbanks, the village created to house workers on the Haweswater dam. It has been written by Liz Hall, from Knipe, whose daughter Sarah achieved literary success with a fictional novel on the subject, entitled Haweswater. Based on real life events, A Lad in Burnbanks is also a drama in true pantomime style.

Cumberland and Westmorland Herald

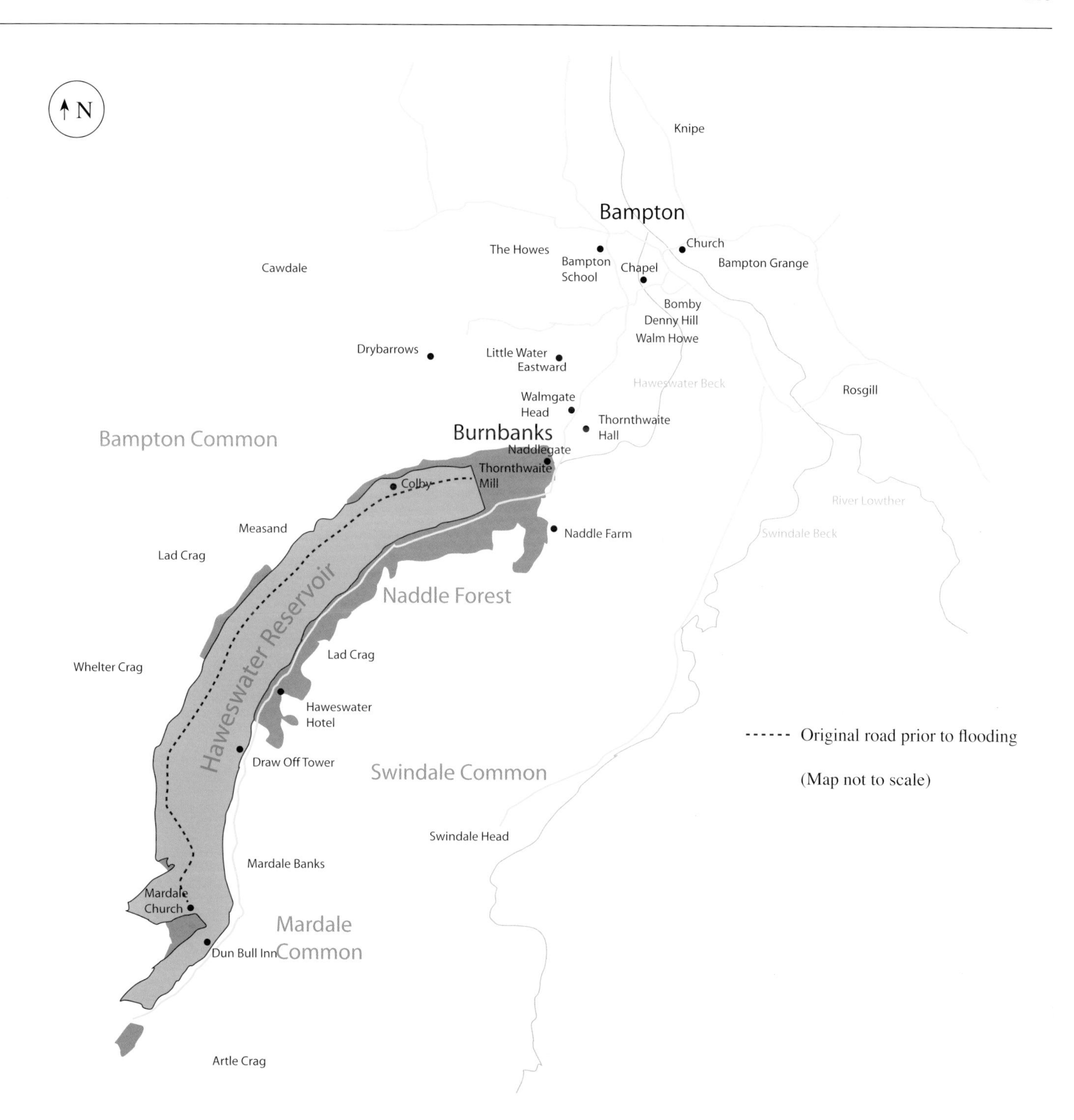
N
Knipe
Bampton
The Howes
Church
Bampton School
Chapel
Bampton Grange
Cawdale
Bomby
Denny Hill
Walm Howe
Drybarrows
Little Water Eastward
Haweswater Beck
Walmgate Head
Rosgill
Thornthwaite Hall
Bampton Common
Burnbanks
Naddlegate
Thornthwaite Mill
Colby
River Lowther
Measand
Naddle Farm
Swindale Beck
Lad Crag
Haweswater Reservoir
Naddle Forest
Whelter Crag
Lad Crag
Haweswater Hotel
Original road prior to flooding
Draw Off Tower
Swindale Common
(Map not to scale)
Swindale Head
Mardale Banks
Mardale Church
Mardale Common
Dun Bull Inn
Artle Crag

Bampton & District Local History Society
www.bampton-history.org.uk